LET'S STUDY
HEBREWS

'Sure-footed, lucid, profound – Hywel Jones' new commentary on Hebrews is all of these. His primary aim throughout, triumphantly achieved, is to help us understand the author's argument for persevering faith in Jesus the Christ. Half a lifetime's reflecting and preaching on the Epistle has been distilled into an exposition which, because it enlightens, is both an encouragement and a challenge.'

EDWARD DONNELLY, Minister of Trinity Reformed Presbyterian Church, Newtownabbey, and Professor of New Testament at Reformed Theological College, Belfast, Northern Ireland.

'Finally – a clear exegetical and practical exposition of the Epistle to the Hebrews for theologians, pastors and lay people. Jones treats *Hebrews* as a letter of profound encouragement to Christians enduring upheaval by turning their eyes to Jesus, the fulfiller of law and prophets, who has blazed a path to heaven where He, as Priest-King, guards and guides all who trust in Him. A masterful study that will help Christians persevere in faith.'

JOEL R. BEEKE, President of Puritan Reformed Theological Seminary and Pastor of the Heritage Netherlands Reformed Congregation in Grand Rapids, Michigan.

Let's Study

HEBREWS

Hywel R. Jones

THE BANNER OF TRUTH TRUST

THE BANNER OF TRUTH TRUST
3 Murrayfield Road, Edinburgh EH12 6EL, UK
P.O. Box 621, Carlisle, PA 17013, USA

*

© Hywel R. Jones 2002
First Published 2002
ISBN 0 85151 814 1

*

*

Typeset in 11/12.5pt Ehrhardt MT at the
Banner of Truth Trust, Edinburgh

Printed in Great Britain by
Bell & Bain Ltd.,
Glasgow

Contents

PUBLISHER'S PREFACE   vii

FOREWORD AND DEDICATION   ix

INTRODUCTION TO THE EPISTLE   x
   1. Authorship   xi
   2. Addressees and Date   xiii
   3. Literary Character and Content   xvi
   4. General Outline and Uses   xxi

PART 1: GOD'S REVELATION AND MAN'S
       RESTORATION (1:1–2:18)   1
   1. Speech and Salvation (1:1–4)   2
   2. Angels over Son? (1:5–14)   9
   3. Pay Full Attention! (2:1–4)   15
   4. Who Rules? (2:5–18)   21

PART 2: JESUS THE APOSTLE AND
       HIGH PRIEST (3:1–10:18)   27
   5. The Household of God (3:1–6)   28
   6. On Pilgrimage (3:7–4:13)   34
   7. A Throne of Grace (4:14–16)   40
   8. Our High Priest (5:1–10)   44
PARENTHESIS (5:11–6:20)   49
   9. Pilgrims' Regress (5:11–6:3)   51
  10. Pilgrims' Relapse (6:4–8)   57
  11. Pilgrims' Progress (6:9–20)   62
  12. Melchizedek and Jesus (7:1–10)   67
  13. Jesus and Aaron (7:11–28)   73

14. A Better Ministry (8:1–6)   80
15. A Better Covenant (8:7–13)   86
16. A Greater Sanctuary (9:1–12)   92
17. A Better Sacrifice (9:13–28)   98
18. Perfected for Ever (10:1–18)   106

PART 3: PERSEVERING FAITH (10:19 – 13:25)   112
19. Keep On Believing (10:19–39)   113
20. One People – One Faith (11:1–2 & 39–40)   119
21. Real Believing (11: 3–7)   124
22. Obtaining Promises (11: 8–38)   129
23. Following the Forerunner (12:1–17)   136
24. In the Kingdom (12:18–29)   142
25. Serving the King at Home (13:1–6)   147
26. Serving the King in the Church (13:7–25)   151

GROUP STUDY GUIDE   157

FOR FURTHER READING   170

Publisher's Preface

Let's Study Hebrews is part of a series of books which explain and apply the message of Scripture. The series is designed to meet a specific and important need in the church. While not technical commentaries, the volumes comment on the text of a biblical book; and, without being merely lists of practical applications, they are concerned with the ways in which the teaching of Scripture can affect and transform our lives today. Understanding the Bible's message and applying its teaching are the aims.

Like other volumes in the series, *Let's Study Hebrews* seeks to combine explanation and application. Its concern is to be helpful to ordinary Christian people by encouraging them to understand the message of the Bible and apply it to their own lives. The reader in view is not the person who is interested in all the detailed questions which fascinate the scholar, although behind the writing of each study lies an appreciation for careful and detailed scholarship. The aim is exposition of Scripture written in the language of a friend, seated alongside you with an open Bible.

Let's Study Hebrews is designed to be used in various contexts. It can be used simply as an aid for individual Bible study. Some may find it helpful to use in their devotions with husband or wife, or to read in the context of the whole family.

In order to make these studies more useful, not only for individual use but also for group study in Sunday School classes and home, church or college, study guide material will be found on pp. 157–69. Sometimes we come away frustrated rather than helped by group discussions. Frequently that is because we have been encouraged to discuss a passage of Scripture which we do not understand very well in the first place. Understanding must

[vii]

always be the foundation for enriching discussion and for thoughtful, practical application. Thus, in addition to the exposition of Hebrews, the additional material provides questions to encourage personal thought and study, or to be used as discussion starters. The Group Study Guide divides the material into thirteen sections and provides direction for leading and participating in group study and discussion.

Foreword and Dedication

The material in this little book has resulted from sermons preached and lectures given on the *Epistle to the Hebrews* over the last thirtry years.

Two churches heard expository addresses on the letter in the course of pastoral ministry. These were Grove Chapel in Camberwell, London, and Borras Park Evangelical Church in Wrexham, Wales. Several other churches, too many to be named, were ministered to from sections of the letter.

Lectures have been given at the Evangelical Movement of Wales Theological Training Course, the London Theological Seminary, the School of the Prophets in Oradea, Romania and also the Puritan and Reformed Theological Seminary in Grand Rapids, Michigan.

The reaction of all these Christians strengthened my conviction of the continuing relevance of the message of this Epistle to the church and I am grateful to the Banner of Truth Trust for its willingness to publish the material in its *Let's Study* series.

Over the years my wife, Nansi, has encouraged me to write up the material and especially during the last months of the task.

I therefore want to dedicate this work to our mothers, Edith Jones (died 1991) and Jennie Jones, who respectively taught each of us the importance of the Bible as the Word of God.

HYWEL R. JONES
Westminster Theological Seminary
in California
January 2002

Introduction
to the Epistle

Imagine that you are in a library. You take down a volume from a shelf and, on opening it, find an old document. You read it, and learn that someone was writing to a group of people whom he knew well, but he does not identify himself or those to whom he was writing. That makes you dissatisfied, but you then realize that you have what the writer wanted the readers to know which, after all, is the main thing. To have a piece of paper with only a 'Dear so and so' at the top and a 'Yours sincerely' at the end cannot be compared with having what lies between them!

This scenario bears some similarities to the *Epistle to the Hebrews* and also to the way in which it should be regarded. The letter has only to be read by anyone with the faintest interest in what it has to say, for something of its importance and value to be perceived. There is, therefore, a sense in which too much should not be made of the fact that it lacks both a signature and an address. This is neither a total loss – because it is the *content* of the letter that matters – nor is it an insuperable hindrance to its being understood – because the letter is not written in code. (After all, its ultimate author is God, the Holy Spirit, and he still speaks by it to the church in every age and place.)

Accepting the letter in this way, however, does not mean that nothing would be gained if the identities of author and addressees were to become known, together with other data like its place of origin, destination and date. These details are usually investigated by way of introduction to the study of a book of the Bible. Sometimes, they can be passed by, because there is no firm evidence about them, but on other occasions discussion is unavoidable because there is material in the actual text which relates directly to such questions. This is the case with *Hebrews*, and so we begin by considering several of its statements, which will help us find our bearings for a study of this letter.

1. 'WHAT MORE SHALL I SAY?' (11:32) – AUTHORSHIP

Although the author refers to himself several times in the letter (see also 13:19, 22–23) and was well known to those whom he addressed, he does not once record his name. This mystery deepens, however, because there was no agreement in the churches of the first three centuries about his identity. In the churches of Egypt and Syria (the East), there was a tradition that Paul was the author, but the churches in Italy, France and Africa (the West), did not think that at all. What is more, even when *Hebrews* was included in the list of recognized New Testament books in the fifth century, no agreement had been reached about its authorship. That was still the case at the time of the sixteenth-century Reformation, and it is so today.

Three factors point strongly in the direction of its *not* being a Pauline letter. They are:

i. *The Epistle is itself anonymous, whereas it was Paul's stated practice, when he had dictated a letter to an amanuensis or assistant, to conclude it in his own hand* (see *2 Thess.* 3:17; *Rom.* 16:22; *Col.* 4:18 and *Philemon* 19). He did this to expose counterfeit letters which were in circulation (see *1 Thess.* 2:2). If Paul had written Hebrews he would not, therefore, have concealed his identity.

Those who favour Pauline authorship argue that, as he was a 'renegade' Jew, it would have been unwise for him to sign it. But this does not fit in with the Epistle to the Galatians where Paul denounces Jewish thinking, and yet he not only uses his own name, but even makes capital out of it in chapter 5:2. In addition, he wrote the whole of that letter himself (see *Gal.* 6:11).

ii. *The structure and style of Hebrews is markedly different from the other Pauline letters in the New Testament.* Paul regularly used the contemporary letter form, namely, greeting, message and farewell; but that is not the pattern of *Hebrews*. In addition, he usually set out the whole of his doctrinal teaching first and then drew from it his practical instruction, whereas in *Hebrews* passages of doctrine are repeatedly interspersed with exhortations. Another factor is that there is a striking contrast between the Greek style of *Hebrews*, which is of a very high literary quality, and that of the Pauline letters.

iii. Finally, *it is very difficult to see how Paul, who made a point of asserting that he had received the gospel message by 'revelation'* (see *Gal.* 1:11,12), *would have said that the gospel was 'confirmed to us by those who heard [the Lord]'* (*Heb.* 2:3).

We therefore conclude that Paul was not the author; but who might he have been? Suggestions have been numerous, but a credible candidate needs to have had close links with Paul, because of the strong Pauline flavour of some statements in the letter. These are: the use of the first person plural to include his companions (see 6: 9,11 and 13:18), a reference to the joyful enduring of persecution (10:34), and a reference to the writer's intention to accompany Timothy on a visit to them (13:23). These are all reminiscent of Paul.

Three individuals have been suggested who meet these criteria, namely *Luke, Barnabas* and *Apollos*. Priscilla (*Acts* 18:26) has also been suggested, but the presence of a masculine participle in the first person statement in 11:32, means that the author must have been male. *Luke* was proposed in the early third century because of the similarities in style between *Hebrews* and *Luke-Acts*, and the suggestion was advanced that he translated into Greek what Paul had written in Hebrew. This solved two problems at once, namely the questions regarding 'style' and authorship; but the similarities between *Hebrews* and *Luke-Acts* are neither numerous enough nor sufficiently substantial to support this possibility.

It was Luther who advocated *Apollos* (*Acts* 18:24–28). There is much to commend that idea and nothing really against it. *Barnabas* (*Acts* 4:36) is another distinct possibility. Either of these would fit the requirements of the letter in terms of its background and style, and also the need for contact with Paul. Both were Greek-speaking Jews and Barnabas was Paul's companion, while Apollos was taught by Priscilla and Aquila, Paul's helpers. Apollos is described in Acts 18:24 as 'an eloquent man' and 'mighty in the Scriptures', and *Hebrews* certainly bears marks of coherent thinking and cogent argument. On the other hand, Barnabas was a Levite, and that fits well with the detail on Old Testament ritual which is found in *Hebrews*, while also harmonizing with its character, since Barnabas was known for his ministry of consolation (*Acts* 4:36). But this is all in the realm of speculation, however attractive these identifications may be. As far back as 225 AD, Origen of Alexandria said, 'But who wrote the Epistle, God only knows certainly.'

Now, some may wonder whether this denial of Pauline authorship diminishes the authority of the letter. Was it not the case in the early Church that the authority of a piece of writing was bound up with the apostolicity of its origin? Yes, it was, but not in the sense that writings had to have apostles for their authors for them to qualify as authentic revelations of the mind of Christ. What of the Gospels of Mark and Luke and the book of the Acts of the Apostles? Known companionship with an apostle was adequate as a formal test of authenticity and, more importantly, so was agreement with apostolic teaching.

The inclusion of *Hebrews* in the New Testament therefore provides an example of how the canon was drawn up. It was by way of response to the effect which sacred literature had on those who heard it. The church's formal acknowledgment of a piece of literature was an 'Amen' to the Holy Spirit's testimony in it, and not a bestowing of its own *imprimatur* and *nihil obstat* upon it.

2. 'THOSE FROM ITALY GREET YOU' (13:24) – ADDRESSEES AND DATE

We are in a somewhat better position with regard to identifying the 'you' in this verse than the 'I' in the verses already referred to. This is because of two factors. First, the letter has a title (*'To the Hebrews'*), which, although it is not corroborated in the actual text, should not be discounted, as it is found in the earliest extant manuscripts. It identifies those addressed as Jewish Christians, although the fact that the author everywhere quoted from the Greek Old Testament, points in the direction of Greek having been their first language. This is the generally accepted view of their identity.

But what else can we discover about them? The quotation with which this section begins tells us that greetings were being sent to them by Italian believers who were in the company of the writer. But where was the writer? Was he in Italy, in which case greetings were being sent from Christians there to brothers and sisters in Judaea, or somewhere else? Or was he in Judaea (or somewhere else) and writing to Christians in Italy, so that Italian Christians sent their greetings home? Neither of these possibilities can be ruled out because people of different nationalities were to be found throughout the Greco-Roman world of the first century. Was the author in *Rome* or *Judaea?* Were those addressed in *Judaea* or *Rome?* Those are the favoured possibilities.

Making a choice between these alternatives is related to another question, namely the *date* of the letter. Clement of Rome, who did not attribute the letter to Paul, showed that he knew of *Hebrews* in a letter which he wrote to Christians in Corinth about 95/96 AD, and so *Hebrews* must have been written before that time. But the real debate is over whether it was more likely to have been written before or after 70 AD, when the destruction of Jerusalem and the Jewish temple by the Romans took place.

A date before 70 AD is much more likely if the letter were written to 'Hebrews' who were living in Judaea. This is because it is very difficult, on a post-70 dating, to make sense of 8:13, which makes clear that the old covenant was about to disappear, and of 9:6–9, 10:1–2 and 13:10, which speak of sacrifices still being offered. Something of this difficulty would still remain even if the letter were written to Jews in Rome, because of the importance of the Jerusalem temple and the provisions of the Sinaitic covenant for Jews everywhere.

We favour a pre-70 dating, in spite of arguments based on 2:3 and 10:32–33. With regard to the time-lapse in 2:3, it is often said that those addressed were 'second-generation Christians'. Although it is not wholly inaccurate to describe them in that way, it is misleading, because it invites a reckoning being made on the basis of the life-span of a generation, and a little bit longer. Doing that would, of course, take one well past 70 AD. But all that is being stated in 2:3 is the difference between receiving information first and second-hand, and that does not require a forty-year interval. It is therefore quite possible, even allowing for the length of time that those addressed have been Christians, to locate the letter before 70 AD. In addition, the sufferings referred to in 10:32–33 did not necessarily occur in the time of Nero, that is, 64–68 AD, even on the basis of the theory that the letter was sent to 'Hebrews' in Rome. The expulsion of Jews referred to in Acts 18:2 (see below) would satisfy this point.

Finally, a pre-70 date neither makes it impossible to accommodate the fact that some leaders had died (see 13:7), nor makes it superfluous to say that Timothy (see 13:23) was still alive – and spiritual declension (see 5:12) can set in with frightening rapidity.

Assuming a pre-70 AD date, what can be said about the destination of the letter? Where were the 'Hebrews?' Currently, the weight of opinion favours Rome as their location. In support of that are the following points. We have seen that the letter was known in Rome about 95 AD, and the *Acts of the Apostles* and *Romans* make clear that there was a decidedly Jewish presence in the churches there (see *Acts* 2:10; 28:15–24 and *Rom.* 14:1–15:7). We also know that Christians were persecuted in Rome as well as Jews (see *Acts* 18:2), and that could be what is in view in 10:32–34. That persecution took place in 49 AD. Hebrews 13:24 could therefore mean, 'Christian Jews in Italy greet you'. But against that is the fact that *Hebrews* was not favoured in Rome, or the West, for some time.

Were they therefore in Jerusalem/Judaea? It is easy to assume that those addressed were in Palestine because of the many references in the letter to Jewish ritual. In addition, we know from *John* and *Acts* that those Jews who were the first converts to Christianity suffered at the hands of their fellow-nationals. That would fit 10:32–34. But the statement that those addressed had not actually heard the Lord, and the facts that the letter is written in polished Greek and that all the Old Testament quotations come from the Septuagint, the Greek version of the Old Testament, cast doubt on this. Even so, a congregation of Hellenistic Jews who had become Christians could have been found somewhere in Judaea.

By way of conclusion to these uncertainties, we can console ourselves with two facts and learn from them. The first is that those who received the letter were well aware, both of who the author was, and of the fact that the letter was meant for them. Similarly, we must regard our possession of this letter as having been directed by the Lord and receive its message as from him.

3. 'BEAR WITH THIS WORD OF EXHORTATION' (13:22) – LITERARY CHARACTER AND CONTENT

The use of the singular, 'word of exhortation', in this verse is significant, because a number of exhortations have just preceded it in the chapter. Coming last it does not add another but summarizes the whole of what was previously written. Although the word translated 'exhortation' can sometimes mean 'encouragement', the verb 'bear with' indicates that such a rendering would be an inappropriate translation at this point. Although positive notes are struck in the letter, and although it ends with an elevating benediction, there are commands and warnings too. It is not incorrect to refer to *Hebrews* as a 'letter', but a more accurate and helpful way of thinking about it is as 'a written word of exhortation'. That says something about its form and its content. We will consider it along those lines.

First, in relation to its *form*, we note that an exhortation is being conveyed by means of 'a letter'. *Hebrews* is therefore one of the epistles of the New Testament. Whenever consideration is being given to these, reference is invariably made to the pattern of letter-writing in the first-century Greco-Roman world. *Hebrews* does not conform to that pattern, as far as its opening is concerned, but its conclusion does contain resemblances to it. However, the Old Testament background to letter writing should also be borne in mind, because it too contains letters, for example Ezra 4:17–23.

Obviously, a letter provided a ready way of communicating with people from a distance. But it also did something else, something which was more important. It brought people together. It did not just deal with the problem of distance between people but also the greater problem of their absence from each other. By means of a letter someone could, therefore, become present to another. This is what the Old Testament shows. It points out that a king could become present to officials in an outpost of his realm, for example, Ezra 4, and that a prophet could become present to people in another country, for example, Jeremiah who wrote a letter to the exiles in Babylon; see Jeremiah 29:1.

A letter, therefore, conveyed a king's edict and a prophet's message and both of those were a word from the Lord. Similarly, in the New Testament, an apostle or teacher could 'become present' to a congregation when his letter was being read to them (see *1 Cor.* 5: 4), and so did the Lord of the church too.

An extra, interesting sidelight is cast on this in the book of Acts. In the synagogue at Antioch, Paul and Barnabas are invited, following the public reading from the Law and the Prophets, to give a 'word of exhortation' to the people (see 13:15). In addition, the content of the letter which summarized the conclusions of the council in Jerusalem, and the ministry of those who commended it, is also described as an exhortation (see 15:31–32).

In the case of *Hebrews*, the writer's exhortation (1:1–13:21) and his brief personal note at the end (13:22–25) were intended as a substitute for his presence until he could come and minister to them in person once more (13:19,23). He was probably one of their current leaders. This is true of the other New Testament letters as well.

It is clear from the text of Hebrews that the author thought of himself as speaking rather than writing, and of those he addressed as his listeners rather than readers (see 2:5; 5:11; 6:9; 8:1; 9:5; 11:32). Because of this, the hortatory element rather than the epistolary style dictated the form of the 'letter'. Writing could therefore convey preaching, and through it all God spoke. *Hebrews* is preaching *via* writing. All New Testament letters, even Philemon and 3 John, are an extension of oral preaching ministry and point to God's living, speaking presence among his people. Holy Scripture is primarily God's message to his church.

But, secondly, in relation to content, we remind ourselves that exhortation is a means of helping people who are in real difficulty. Why did the 'Hebrews' need help and how did the writer aim to provide it? This is another way of asking the old question, 'Why was Hebrews written and what did its author have to say?' As the Greek word for 'exhortation' relates closely to the term 'Paraclete', which designates the Holy Spirit in his ministry to believers (*John* 14: 16), we can ask, What was the Holy Spirit saying in and through the letter? By bringing God's truth in Christ to believers and impressing it on their minds and hearts, the Holy Spirit expresses his care and imparts his strength. *Hebrews* is an explicit and urgent exhortation from the Spirit of God. We will look first at the need for exhortation and then at its content.

I. *THE NEED FOR THE EXHORTATION*

Wherever these Jewish Christians lived, the important fact is that they were professing Christians. That is incontestable and we will have to refer to it repeatedly as we consider what is said about them.

It is clear from the closing part of the letter that they formed a distinct group and that they gathered together for worship and fellowship (10:25). They had their own leaders, who succeeded the founders of the church (13:17,7). Given the details in 13:1–14, they probably lived in a large town or city, and there were other Christians in their general vicinity (see 13:24).

What is disclosed about their need is presented by means of a review of their history as Christian people. Certain terms are used to describe their past and present, and to explore their future. Their Christian beginnings are referred to as 'the former days' (10:32), and the interval between that and the writing of the letter by the words, 'for the time' (5:12). That stands for their past. Their present is indicated by the repeated use of 'Today' (3:7–4:9) and what is said about their current condition. Their future is described in connection with 'the day approaching'(10:25) and what that involves.

What the writer is wanting to bring to their notice is the dissimilarity between their present condition and their past, and, on that basis, to provoke serious thought about their future.

'The Former Days'

As has been pointed out, they had heard the good news of God's 'so great a salvation' from those who had heard the Lord Jesus Christ; they had seen the miraculous signs by which God had confirmed the authenticity of the message and the messengers (2:3–4) and had confessed faith in Jesus as their 'Apostle and High Priest' (3:1). This was as a result of light from above having been graciously given to them (10:32).

They were no strangers to suffering. Scorn and loss in no small measure crossed their path. Joyful expectation of heavenly glory and gain invigorated them. When they could, conceivably, have enjoyed some respite, they laid themselves out for other believers who were being persecuted (10:32–34). By such exertions they had displayed brotherly love, brave faith and confident hope in God (6:10) and showed that they could indeed be called 'holy brethren, partakers of a heavenly calling' (3:1).

'Today'

But a change had set in and their condition was no longer what it had been. Indolence was at the root of their decline, as sluggishness is twice specified in 5:11–14, where a diagnosis of their current condition is presented. The imagery of the gymnasium is used in verse 14 to point out, by contrasting implication, that the Hebrews had not been engaging in daily 'work-outs', but had become 'layabouts'. It was a case of pilgrims' regress and not pilgrims' progress. There are many calls to action in the letter – the exact opposite of the malaise which had set in. They are compared to a ship which is drifting wherever the current may take it (2:1).

They should have become teachers, but instead they needed to be retaught what once they knew (5:11-12). Instead of having cut their teeth on God's solid truth, they were back on the diet of infants. As a result, they were unable to pay attention to the Word of God properly (5:11), and to live strongly and expectantly in the light of it. Confidence had waned (3:6,14; 6:11; 10: 23, 35–36). The practices of other religions, together with their teachings, were constituting a danger to them (13:9–10). The prospect of further and more severe suffering made them more than apprehensive. 'Today' – the day in which God was repeating his word and renewing his call to them through it – was a time in which the Hebrews had become 'hard of hearing'. Their plight was serious.

'The Day Drawing Near'

A more critical day, however, was approaching. The terse way in which this is designated means that no further description of it is needed in order for it to be identified. In the Old Testament, 'the day' would be 'the day of the LORD', when he would personally intervene; in the New, it is the day when the Lord Jesus will return (see comment on 10:25). If the Hebrews ought to heed God's Word, which they had been told and which he was still speaking to them, 'all the more' (10:25) ought they to do so, because on the day of the Lord's return, their response would reap everlasting consequences. Persevering would be rewarded but drawing back would be punished (10:35–39).

This is why, alongside the many encouragements which are given in the letter to persevere, for example, 'to pay closer attention', 'to hold fast', 'to be diligent', 'to draw near', 'to press on', 'to encourage one another', and the like, there are severe warnings in terms of their opposites. There is the danger of 'drifting', of 'being hardened', and most seriously 'departing', 'drawing back' and 'sinning defiantly'. Apostasy is irreversible.

It was in the light of all these considerations that this letter was written. The Hebrews were at a critical stage in their spiritual history. But what did the writer have to say to them?

II. *The Content of the Exhortation*

What the writer has to say to them is related to another use of the noun 'day'. He wants to make it clear to them that they are living in a period which he calls '[the] last days' (1:2). He sees the beginning of all things as marked by the creation, and their end by the incarnation of Christ (9:26), which has, of course, already taken place. Christians are therefore living on the borders of eternity. This is the 'age to come' (2:5). All he has to say to them relates to what characterizes this era whose hallmark, so to speak, is that the Messiah has come and 'so great a salvation' is available. This is the answer to their need.

This era is a time of glorious privilege. But it is a serious time too, because, unlike the old (Sinaitic) covenant which preceded it, there is nothing temporary about the New Covenant. It is unshakeable (12:27–28). It will not be succeeded by another. To reject it – especially after professing to receive it – leaves one in a worse position than those who rejected the Mosaic covenant. There is no other sacrifice for sin (9:26) and no other way to escape the awesome judgment of God (2:3; 10:28–31).

Jesus the Christ who is ever 'the same' is therefore to be the focus of Christians' persevering trust. The Apostle and High Priest *par excellence* has come (3:1). Like Moses and Joshua (3:2; 4:8) he is sent by God, but he brings the rest which they could not give. Like Aaron, but more like Melchizedek (5:1–10; 6:20 – 10:18), he rules because he actually deals with sin and its consequences. This supplies the logic for the repeated use of the comparative adjective 'better' (see 1:4; 7:19,22; 8:6; 9:23; 10:34; 11:16,35) with reference to a name, hope, covenant, promises, sacrifices, substance, country and resurrection. Jesus Christ brings in something altogether better than the old, preparatory era could actually provide (11:40).

The last days are the era between the two comings of the Lord Jesus Christ (9:28). It is a glorious time to be living in. By his first coming, he accomplished atonement and, in heaven, intercedes for those for whom he lived and died. Through him there is open entry into God's presence (10:19); mercy and grace are available (4:16) and salvation 'to the uttermost' for all who keep coming to God (7:25). There is help to keep looking to him and to keep running the race (12:1–2) – to keep on believing, as did many before he came and as he did himself. There is therefore no excuse for not persevering. He will neither be ashamed of his pilgrim people nor forget and fail them.

4. GENERAL OUTLINE AND USES

'Therefore . . . consider Jesus, the Apostle and High Priest of our confession' (3:1), is arguably the text of this written sermon. It contains the three main themes of the letter namely Jesus as Apostle and as High Priest and the duty of confessing him in persevering faith.

But the sermon 'text' begins with the word 'therefore'. This means that, like every good sermon, it has an introduction which, in this case, is the opening two chapters of the letter. These deal with the self-revelation of God and with his restoration of the universe and mankind which sin had marred. That is the background against which Jesus the Apostle and High Priest is to be considered. In him God has spoken finally, and is ruling redemptively.

Finally, 'our text' calls for a response. It is twofold. First, a consideration of Jesus is called for, and secondly, an ongoing confession of faith.

i. OUTLINE

Chapters 1 and 2:   The doctrinal setting – God revealed and Man restored

Chapter 3:1– 4:13: Jesus the Apostle – Superior to Moses and Joshua
Chapter 4:14–10:18: Jesus the High Priest – Superior to Aaron and Melchizedek
Chapter 10:19–13:25: Hold fast to him and follow him – alone!

Confess him in persevering faith

ii. *USES*

While the content of this letter was relevant to those initially addressed, it also has a direct bearing on several pressure points in the life of the Christian and the church today. Mentioning some of these at the outset will have the benefit of alerting the student to material in the book that is particularly important. Among these are the following, which we put in question form so as to provoke thought on these issues.

a. *In relation to the Bible,* is the Old Testament as much the Word of God as the New? Is it a 'Christian' book? If so, how can it be properly understood?

b. *In relation to our multi-faith context,* what is the relation between Judaism and Christianity? Is the one as valid as the other? If not, what about other religions in relation to Christianity?

c. *In relation to the death of Jesus Christ,* what is its meaning? Is it essential or unimportant? Can it be repeated in any sense? Does it need to be?

d. *In relation to faith,* what is actually involved in believing? Is it merely a decision of the intellect or the will or is it something more? How important is persevering to the end?

e. *In relation to the church,* how important are the character of Christian worship, the preaching of the Word, praise and prayer, and how Christians care for one another?

PART 1

God's Revelation
and Man's Restoration
(1:1 – 2:18)

By an all-creative word, God conferred on man a place of supremacy in the world that he had made through his eternal Son, commanding him to rule over it for his glory.

Man sinned, lost that dignity and jeopardized that destiny. But by a redemptive word in the same Son, now an individual and representative human, God is restoring man to that standing and usefulness.

I

Speech and Salvation

GOD, after He spoke long ago to the fathers in the prophets in many portions and in many ways, [2] in these last days has spoken to us in His Son, whom He appointed heir of all things, through whom also He made the world. [3] And He is the radiance of His glory and the exact representation of His nature, and upholds all things by the word of His power. When He had made purification of sins, He sat down at the right hand of the Majesty on high; [4] having become as much better than the angels, as He has inherited a more excellent name than they (Heb. 1:1–4).

In any study of this letter these verses are generally isolated and considered together. This is because, whether the author intended it or not, they seem to provide a very natural introduction to all that follows. They do this in three respects. First, the emphasis on God's self-disclosure provides the foundation and the framework for all that the letter contains. Secondly, focusing attention on the divine Son is characteristic of the whole letter. Thirdly, the mention of the angels connects with the rest of the opening two chapters. We will consider these matters in that order.

1. 'GOD . . . HAS SPOKEN' (verses 1 and 2a)
Two eras of divine self-disclosure are referred to in these verses. What marks each off from the other is the coming and ministry of 'a Son'. They can therefore be roughly equated with our Old and New Testaments. Although there are several differences between them that must not be overlooked, there is also something common to them which is most important. It is that they are equally God's

#1
↓

speech, that is his self-revelation. The fact that the God who had spoken has spoken once more is asserted in each of these two verses. That is what binds them together. What differentiates them relates to the 'when and how' of God's speaking.

Speech is only possible for someone who has life, and that means more than having existence. God speaks because he 'is' (11:6) and he is 'the living God' (3:12 and 9:14). He can therefore reveal himself, if he chooses to do so, and because he is light and love he delights to make himself known. He is not the kind of deity who keeps himself to himself and lets people blunder on in their darkness. He 'speaks' or better he 'talks' (the word in the original text is the term for human conversation). God comes near to his human creatures and converses with them rather than declaims from on high. The Bible is God saying, 'Here I am', and, 'This is the way' (see *Isa.* 45:18–25). ←

Read aloud

What is more, the God who speaks cannot lie (6:18) and so he keeps his promises which express his vows and desires (6:13 and 17). He responds with an open hand to those who seek him (11:6b), but he also executes his threats against those who 'refuse' to hear his voice (12:25). His words have been recorded, and yet, because he is alive, he still speaks through them (4:7 – note present tense here and elsewhere).

One and the same God is therefore revealed in both Testaments and binds them together. Consequently, we must not pit them against each other. There is a harmony between them. Even so, they are not to be equated. There are important differences between them and the opening two verses set these out by way of four contrasts. The first is highlighted by the couplet *'long ago'* and *'in these last days'*. The next couplet is *'in the prophets'* and *'in a Son'*. The third contrast relates to *'in many portions and in many ways'* and to the opposite of that, which is implicit in the mention of *'a Son'*. Finally, there is the contrast between *'to the fathers'* and *'to us'*. We will consider each of these in turn.

i. *'Long ago . . . these last days'.*

These are descriptions of eras of divine self-revelation; phases in God's speaking to men. They are not just chronological references. 'Distant' and 'recent' would not be adequate substitutes for them;

nor would 'then' and 'now'. The author's use of the demonstrative adjective 'these' indicates that the first era is past, and that the second has begun and is current. PAST and CURRENT

But his choice of the expression 'last days' is borrowed from that earlier revelation which described what lay ahead in the purpose of God by terms such as 'the latter days', or 'the last day', or 'afterwards' (see *Num.* 24:14). 'These last days' is therefore not an era which is completely novel in character. It had been fore-shadowed and anticipated in the earlier era. 'Long ago' is therefore the era of prediction and preparation which, though past, is not irrelevant; the 'last days' are the era of fulfilment and finality.

#2

ii. *'By the prophets . . . in a Son'.*

This contrast specifies God's spokesmen in the eras just mentioned. 'Prophets' are related to 'long ago', the era marked by prediction and preparation. 'A Son' belongs to the 'last days', the era of fulfilment. But all are spokesmen, because divine communication necessarily involves divine condescension. For God – the word refers to all that distinguishes deity – to speak to man is a stupendous act of sheer grace on his part. Man is dependent on God's Word for knowledge of him and his ways.

There are two aspects to this contrast which present the major difference between the Testaments. The first relates to the fact that there are (many) prophets but (only) one Son; the second is the contrast between them as human and him as divine. We will consider the second first because it will explain the other aspect.

It is important to remember that in these verses the human prophets and the divine Son are being differentiated as messengers of God. What is implicit in the term 'Son' is described in what immediately follows. We therefore narrow our inquiry to what sets a prophet apart from a Son as a messenger of God. John the Baptist dealt with this matter when he contrasted himself, the greatest of the prophets, with Jesus, the Son of God (see *John* 3:25–36 and especially verses 31–34.) He made clear that a prophet is 'from the earth and speaks of the earth' whereas the Son is 'from above' and speaks 'what he has seen and heard'. There is therefore a vast difference between them in terms of the vantage-point from which they view and declare divine things.

The prophet is given to see these from below (from afar and in part), and gives testimony to them in human terms. The Son, who is from above, hears the words and sees the works of God by virtue of intimate and immediate communion with God, his Father, and he declares them and does them.

There is therefore a fullness and a finality about God's self-revelation in a Son which *cannot* characterize the ministry of any prophet. Given this difference, it is easy to understand why there were many prophets but only one Son. Not one of them – nor all of them together – could match 'a Son' as a messenger for truth known and declared.

iii. *'In many portions and in many ways . . .'*

There is no expression in the text in direct contrast with the above words. What contrasts with their meaning is implicit in the mention of 'a Son'. They describe how the revelation which was given 'long ago' and 'in the prophets' was given (necessarily) 'in many portions and in many ways'.

The different 'portions' in which revelation was given covered the time-span of fifteen centuries or so. Sometimes, it was rapidly augmented, for example in the eighth to sixth centuries BC with the major prophets. But it seemed to be at a standstill, for example, before the call of Abram, or to have come to a final end after Malachi. The different 'ways' may relate either to the several means by which revelation was given to the prophets, or to the different amounts of truth that they communicated. Both apply because all the prophets were but human. The Old Testament therefore exhibits that variety and progression which lay within God's self-revelation. It was not the result of human development or discovery but was intended to lead people step by step to the Son.

While Moses was admitted into greater intimacy with Jehovah than other prophets (see *Num.* 12:6–8), even he did not see the LORD face to face (see *Exod.* 33:18–23). The prophets were human. Not one of them, not even Isaiah, who saw the pre-incarnate Son (*John* 12:38), could bear the burden or bring the truth which the Son himself could. Being finite imposed limitations on what the prophets could receive and declare at any one time, and God graciously fitted in with this. The Son is not subject to any such impediment. He is 'from above' and is the Truth.

iv. *'To the fathers . . . to us'.*

This contrast completes the picture and it sounds a practical note. The author's aim is not to give his readers a crash course in the relationship between the two eras of revelation in order to make them budding theologians. His concern is to make sure that they realize where they fit into the divine scheme of things and to whom they are to listen. Long ago God spoke by prophets to the fathers; now the same God is speaking by his Son 'to us'. He is therefore the one to whom *special* attention is to be paid – not the prophets. The present era of revelation is far more important than the previous one.

2. 'IN HIS SON' (verses 2b and 3)

The uniqueness of 'his Son' is now unfolded. He is God's Revealer and his Redeemer. There is no possessive pronoun 'his' in the original text and no definite article. But a 'Son' does not mean one among others, but a Son *indeed*. The absence of a definite article thus points to the character of the noun. The uniqueness of his sonship is spoken of from three perspectives: first, in relation to all created things; second, in relation to God's own glory and nature, and third, in relation to human sin.

i. *In relation to 'all things' and 'the worlds'* – He is their divinely appointed creator, upholder and owner (heir).

Nothing that exists is to be excluded from this category. The plural noun 'worlds' reflects the way Jews thought and spoke about things unseen as well as seen. The majestic statements of Colossians 1:15–23; John 1:1–3; Proverbs 8: 22–24 and the whole of Genesis 1:1–2:3 are all relevant at this point.

Because every single thing is made, nothing is self-derived. What is more it is not self-perpetuating. It needs to be upheld, and consequently it belongs to the one who gave it existence and maintains it. It is his inheritance. The Son does all this by God's appointment. The implication therefore is that he himself antedates all that has come into being.

[6]

ii. *In relation to the glory and nature of God* – He is his radiance and replica.

Two important terms are used here which are not found anywhere else in the New Testament. They are translated 'radiance' and 'representation'. We consider them, on the basis that they are complementary rather than synonymous terms. 'Radiance' stresses the Son's oneness with God; 'exact representation' his 'otherness' to God.

a. *The Son is the 'radiance' of God's glory.*

'Someone revealed by something', is a good working definition of the term 'glory' in the Bible. The glory of God is therefore a display of what is unique to him. As his 'radiance', the Son does not reflect that glory as the moon does that of the sun, but is the very beam of the divine brightness breaking into our dark world. The Shekinah glory of the Old Testament (see *Exod.* 40:34–38) lies in the mind of the writer at this point.

b. *The Son is the 'exact representation of [God's] nature'.*

Not all that is true of God is revealed in a particular display of his glory. The universe (only) displays his wisdom and power but human beings show by their conscience and conduct that God is also moral (*Rom.* 1:20; 2:14–16). However, revelation in a Son reveals more than even all that.

The allusion in the term rendered 'exact representation' is to the image produced by a die on a seal, or a coin. The outline of the die corresponds to the imprint on the image produced. The one can therefore be seen in the other. God's 'nature' is his essence which is invisible and unknowable to human beings on earth. The Son is therefore the *alter ego* of God in an exact way and to a complete degree.

iii. *In relation to human sin and its consequences* – He is its conqueror.

Compressed into this statement are many aspects of truth that will be treated at length in the body of the letter. But there are outlines here which are important. First, 'the Son' himself had to do something more than create and uphold the universe in order to deal with sin. Secondly, what was necessary in that regard is described in terms borrowed from the world of Old Testament sacrificial ritual and priestly activity. 'To purify' is a term that relates to an altar and to people, that is to God and to human beings, but not in the same way. It speaks of God as offended and of people as defiled. Thirdly, it was only after he had atoned for sin to the satisfaction of 'the Majesty on high', that he could be enthroned as ruler over all.

3. 'HAVING BECOME SO MUCH BETTER THAN THE ANGELS' (verse 4).

The kind of superiority over the angels which is spoken of in this verse is one that the Son gained as a result of his atoning work, which resulted in his enthronement at God's right hand. That conferred on him a 'better name' than angels possessed. He became God's vicegerent over all; he became Lord.

But in verse 5 the writer speaks about 'Son' and 'being begotten'. Does this not refer to his eternal Sonship? No, it does not. Much less does it prove that he 'became' Son by virtue of the incarnation and his birth of Mary at Bethlehem. He was 'Son' from all eternity, not only 'Word', or God could not have been an eternal Father.

The kind of sonship which is in view is Messianic. It is in keeping with the times predicted in 2 Samuel 7:12. By virtue of his having been begotten of the Father before the worlds were made he was God's eternal Son; it was by virtue of an obedient life and an atoning death that he became God's kingly messiah.

But why did the writer introduce this comparison with angels, which is a recurring note in the first two chapters of this Epistle? The answer lies in the thought-world of those he was addressing. Jews had an excessively high regard for angels. They saw them as connected with the most significant events in their religious and national history, namely the giving of the law (see 2:2; *Acts* 7:53 and *Gal.* 3:19) and the deliverance from Egypt (*Exod.* 3:2 and *Isa.* 63:9). Angels were therefore bound up with revelation (Sinai) and redemption (The Passover). The writer says, in effect, that however important angels are, or prophets for that matter, the Son exceeds them all. He is divine revelation and redemption, incarnate and final, and is therefore to be more highly esteemed than they. That is what is proved in the following section.

2

Angels over Son?

⁵For to which of the angels did He ever say, 'Thou art My Son, Today I have begotten Thee'? And again, 'I will be a Father to Him, and He shall be a Son to Me'? ⁶ And when He again brings the first-born into the world, He says, 'And let all the angels of God worship Him.' ⁷ And of the angels He says, 'Who makes His angels winds, and His ministers a flame of fire.' ⁸ But of the Son He says, 'Thy throne, O God, is forever and ever, and the righteous scepter is the scepter of His kingdom. ⁹ Thou hast loved righteousness and hated lawlessness; therefore God, Thy God, hath anointed Thee with the oil of gladness above Thy companions.' ¹⁰ And, 'Thou, Lord, in the beginning didst lay the foundation of the earth, and the heavens are the works of Thy hands; ¹¹ They will perish, but Thou remainest; and they all will become old as a garment, ¹² and as a mantle Thou wilt roll them up; as a garment they will also be changed. But Thou art the same, and Thy years will not come to an end.' ¹³ But to which of the angels has He ever said, 'Sit at My right hand, until I make Thine enemies a footstool for Thy feet'? ¹⁴ Are they not all ministering spirits, sent out to render service for the sake of those who will inherit salvation? (Heb. 1:5–14).

It is always important to give priority to the Old Testament in studying any part of the New Testament and that, of course, applies particularly to the *Epistle to the Hebrews*. The writer of this letter makes frequent use of the Old Testament. He does so in two ways; by alluding to its contents and by quoting its texts. Allusions abound in the verses which have already been examined where people, events and even texts (for example, Psalm 110 is the background to verse 3b) are in view. Such a wealth of material is woven together seamlessly with the new revelation. This not only shows the writer's mastery of the Old Testament but also its own harmony with the revelation 'in a Son'. The Old Testament is a 'Christian' book.

In these verses, however, there are actual quotations – seven of them. Before we consider them in turn, we ought to give some thought to the fact that they do not agree in every detail with their counterparts in the Old Testament. How can this discrepancy be explained? Considering this at the outset will hopefully settle some difficulties and also highlight some important truths which affect the whole letter.

1. THE TEXT OF THE QUOTATIONS.

Before any New Testament book had been written, the Hebrew Old Testament had been translated into Greek (the Septuagint). Jews had been scattered throughout the Roman Empire and there were synagogues in many places. Greek became their first language and the Septuagint was their 'Bible'. This is reflected in the use made of it by several New Testament writers, the author of *Hebrews* included.

Our writer used both forms of the Old Testament text, Hebrew and Greek. There is an example of his use of the Septuagint in the quotation that he makes in verse 6, 'Let all the angels of God worship him.' These words probably come from Psalm 97:7 which in Hebrew has 'gods' instead of 'angels'. However, this does not mean that the author of *Hebrews* falsified the psalmist's original meaning because the Hebrew for 'gods' can mean 'angels'. Other New Testament writers made similar adjustments when they did not quote verbatim from the Old Testament, or when they combined texts from different parts of it. The same applies to comments made by way of introduction to material about to be quoted (see below). Being divinely inspired and following the Spirit's leading, their use of Old Testament material is in accord with its intended meaning.

2. THE PREFACE TO THE QUOTATIONS.

What identifies a number of words as a quotation is that they are introduced by a prefacing comment. The verses before us contain a selection of these, but there are also others in the rest of the letter. Two things need to be said in connection with them.

i. The prefaces in 1:5–14, even the seemingly innocuous words *'and again'*, indicate that the quotations introduced are being made as part of an argument that is being presented. The point of that argument is the Son's superiority over the angels and each of the seven quotations in this section is geared to that truth. This is a good example of the fact that, whenever a New Testament writer employs an Old Testament text, he does so with a particular aim in view, and that aim is often to highlight some aspect of the glory of Christ. This messianic or Christ-centred use of the Old Testament is a proper understanding of it. In all its parts it speaks of him (*Luke* 24:27, 44).

ii. It is a surprising fact that nowhere does the author of *Hebrews* use the verb 'to write' to introduce an Old Testament quote. The words, 'as it is written', occur regularly elsewhere, especially in the Gospels. But in *Hebrews* we find the verb 'to say', and it occurs in the present tense, meaning he or it *'says'*, not *'has said'*. That is explicitly the case in verses 6 and 7 and it is understood in verses 8 and 10. When other tenses are used, for example in verses 5 and 13, they are necessitated by the flow of the writer's argument.

It is this present tense of the verb 'to say' which is unique to this letter. As the author writes, he is thinking about the Old Testament in terms either of what God 'says' or what the text 'says'. Either way, his view of the Old Testament is dynamic. The one who spoke it, so that it could be recorded, is the one who still speaks in and by it. The writer even refers to the Son and to the Spirit as 'speaking' Old Testament Scripture in 2:12–13 and 3:7–11. The Old Testament is vibrant speech and not just verbal record. 'The word of God is living' (4:12).

But this emphasis does not mean that he is unaware or dismissive of the fact that human beings wrote the Scriptures. In 4:7 he writes, 'saying through David', as he quotes from Psalm 95, and in 9:20 he attributes Exodus 24:8 to Moses. When he writes 'someone, somewhere' in 2:6, as he quotes from Psalm 8, and in 4:4 where he quotes from Genesis 2:2, he is neither indicating ignorance of detail nor being casual. He knows who said it, and where it was recorded – and more to the point, he knows that his readers know too! This choice of words on his part is geared to prompting his readers to fill in the gaps from their memory so that they will recall who the real speaker was and why he said what he did!

3. The Meaning of the Quotations in 1:5–14

The seven quotations which are employed are derived from Psalm 2:7; 2 Samuel 7:14; Deuteronomy 32:43 or Psalm 97:7; Psalm 104:4; Psalm 45:6; Psalm 102:25–27 and Psalm 110:1. Listing the references in this way has the advantage of drawing attention to the fact that the Psalter is heavily used – as it is later in the letter. Those addressed would be familiar with the Psalter from their upbringing and participation in the services at the synagogue.

All these quotations consist of words spoken by the Father to his Son which confirm the designations given to him in verses 2 and 3, and also mark him off from all the angels. They demonstrate what is meant by the Son's having a name that angels do not possess, and they build up a case for his superiority. We will consider each step of the argument in order.

i. *Verse 5 provides the foundation for all that follows.* It combines two remarks from Psalm 2:7 and 2 Samuel 7:14. Kingship is the dominant theme in each of these and not sonship. The king is described as a son and not *vice versa*. In Psalm 2, God sets his king over the nations. In 2 Samuel a king is promised of David's line who will build a house for God (see *Heb.* 3:6 and 10:21). The reference to 'today' and to 'begotten' points to an enthronement and not to a pre-temporal begetting. That is how the apostle Paul interpreted the statement in Acts 13:33. He saw it as a prediction of the resurrection of the Messiah, the beginning of his exaltation. Both verses therefore predict a messianic kingship, and in his preface the writer simply underlines the fact that a promise of such a kingship was not made to any of the angels. God's king is a 'Royal-Son' and not a created angel.

ii. *Verse 6 is addressed to the angels, but it is about the Son.* It quotes from the Greek Septuagint translation, either of Deuteronomy 32: 43 or of Psalm 97: 7. Each of these is a divine word addressed to angels. The Hebrew text in the Psalm has 'gods', but, as mentioned already, that can be another term for angels. They are called upon to worship God who (from the perspective of the text) is going to come into his world to judge and bless. Worship is always the duty of the lesser to the greater. Angels are therefore subordinate to God.

But it is *'the firstborn'* whom they are to worship. The firstborn was someone who had a higher rank and a special inheritance in the family. The introduction of this term continues the emphasis of kingship, because David was God's 'firstborn' (see *Psa.* 89:27). The *2 Sam.* 7 passage, which speaks of an eternal reign of a son of David, lies in the background here, referring to the Messiah whom God would bring into the world. One other detail should be noted. We have been emphasizing that the sonship which is referred to in these verses is not the eternal sonship of the Second Person of the Trinity but is 'a kingship for God', typified by David who as 'God's son' was to reign over all. (In the next chapter it will be Adam: see also *Luke* 3:38; *Gen.* 5:1–3 and 1:28). Even so, the one to be worshipped in the Deuteronomy and Psalm texts is Jehovah. In Hebrews it is the Son. The conclusion is inescapable. The Son is fully divine.

iii. *Verses 7–9 contrasts the royal Son and the angels.* Verse 7 quotes from Psalm 104: 4, which celebrates Jehovah's sovereign rule over all created things and natural processes, including angels and their activities. Angels therefore are Jehovah's ministers, his servants in the execution of his providential purposes. Verses 8–9, standing in contrast with verse 7, quote from Psalm 45, which exults prophetically in the triumph of Jehovah's king over his enemies and his marriage to his people. This king sits on a throne, is addressed as God (by Jehovah), is a perfect king for God (a man after God's own heart in all respects) and is rewarded with the gift of the Spirit for his people whom he takes into union with himself.

iv. *Verses 10–12 contain no specific reference to either 'angel' or 'Son'.* But it is the Son who is being addressed, as is made clear by the simple conjunction at the beginning of verse 10 which indicates a continuation from verse 8. The quotation is from Psalm 102:25–27 in which the eternity and immutability of Jehovah, the creator, are being contrasted with the transience of all things created. All that is now predicated of the Son.

v. *Verse 13, which quotes from Psalm 110:1, is addressed to the Son-King of David who is given universal sway.* The prefacing comment of the writer underlines that such a position was not given to any angel. Rather, all angels are servants of this royal king and accomplish his beneficent designs. As 'spirits', they are incorporeal beings created by the Son; as ministers (servants) they perform his commands. They are therefore dependent upon him and subservient to him. Far from being superior to him they are not even superior to believers, because they stoop to serve them, protecting, guiding and strengthening them according to the directives of the Son.

The Son is therefore King, not only over creation, but also over the church. He is therefore infinitely higher than the angels in both the natural and the spiritual realms. He has no equal in the purpose of God and is therefore to have no rival in the esteem of his people.

3

Pay Full Attention!

For this reason we must pay much closer attention to what we have heard, lest we drift away from it. ² For if the word spoken through angels proved unalterable, and every transgression and disobedience received a just recompense, ³ how shall we escape if we neglect so great a salvation? After it was at the first spoken through the Lord, it was confirmed to us by those who heard, ⁴ God also bearing witness with them, both by signs and wonders and by various miracles and by gifts of the Holy Spirit according to His own will (Heb. 2:1–4).

This is the first of several 'warning passages' contained in this letter (see also 3:6b–4:12; 5:11–6:8; 10:26–31; 12:15–17 and 25–29). While every effort must be made not to diminish their seriousness, it does need to be remembered that their aim, like all apostolic instruction, is 'edification and not destruction' (*2 Cor.* 10:8). They are neither heartless threats nor self-fulfilling prophecies. They are an exhortation which is truly evangelical in spirit and content.

Two things should be noticed from the way in which this preacher writes. First, he moves with great ease from the doctrinal and exegetical exposition contained in chapter 1 to the kind of vocabulary and style which are required for application of his message. This provides a good model for preachers. In exhortation, vocabulary should be simple and graphic; style should be lucid and direct.

Secondly, an exhortation is not a feverish appeal for frantic activity. It is a call for specific action, motivated by understanding. Its force is derived from its being grounded in truth – not in the charisma or eloquence of the preacher. In this exhortation, our author-preacher states clearly the basis, character and purpose of his appeal in verse 1 and then enlarges on it in verses 2–4. That is how we will consider these verses.

1. THE EXHORTATION STATED

Its Basis – 'Therefore'.

This word is of considerable significance whenever it is used in the Bible. It shows that what follows arises from what has already been said and that those addressed should appreciate the logic of the connection. Christianity or true spirituality is not irrational. It is because the Son is superior to prophets and angels as a revealer of God that the 'what we have heard' commands such attention. Christian faith is not blind and Christian obedience is not mindless.

Its Nature – 'Much closer attention'.

The comparative adjective 'closer' not only points in the direction of what is appropriate by way of response to this greater revelation; it also focuses on the inadequate degree of attentiveness which the Hebrews had been paying to it. The fact that the writer does not use the superlative degree – 'closest' – does not mean that he envisages that a greater degree of attentiveness is to be reserved for something else. As we have seen, he is thinking of the two eras of divine speech. Thus his 'better' means 'best', and 'much closer attention' therefore means something like 'full attention'. In addition, the verb translated 'we must pay' is in the present tense, which means that something ongoing and never completed in this life is in view. What is more, this attention is not optional. The word 'must' is so insistent and unyielding. Later on (see 5:11) the writer will accuse them of spiritual indolence and inertia.

The Purpose – 'Lest we drift away'.

Although the writer's aim is positive, namely that his readers will come to possess 'the full assurance of hope' (6:11), he pursues it negatively in this verse by means of a wake-up call to danger. He depicts a ship on the high seas which is at the mercy of wind and tide unless sailors 'take heed' – a word elsewhere meaning to drop anchor in the storm, or to hold the ship on a steady bearing towards port. The Hebrews are exposed to forces that will carry them away from what they have heard unless they repeatedly make efforts to counter them. Doing nothing will result in the loss of everything.

2. THE EXHORTATION ENLARGED – verses 2–4

Every good preacher should be able to state things as succinctly as our writer has done; but no preacher worth his salt is content with doing only that. He knows that things have to be unpacked for his hearers, because they may fail to appreciate their importance. That is what the author does in these verses. He wants them to realize the importance of what they have heard and the danger of not adhering to it. So, he gives them an analogy.

He reminds them of what happened to those who did not give proper attention to what they heard in Old Testament days. This provides him with a platform for going on to show that something far worse is bound to happen to all who react in the same way to the greater message they have heard. The argument from the lesser to the greater here is very forceful.

The 'word spoken through angels'.

This is a reference to the giving of the law at Sinai which constituted the tribes of Israel as the people of God. Jews believed that angels were involved in this and there are statements in Old Testament poetry to this effect (see *Deut.* 33:2 and *Psa.* 68:17). Even so, angels were only instruments, acting at God's command. But this revelation, though only anticipatory, had divine validity. It was therefore not to be treated disrespectfully. 'Transgression and disobedience' are ways of describing sins of omission and commission. Every kind of infringement of this 'word' was treated seriously by God, and all who set it aside received a just retribution. Examples of this are found in Exodus 32: 6, 28; Leviticus 10:1–2; Numbers 15:32, 36; 16:3, 32, 35 and 20:12 and 34.

'So great a salvation'.

Contrasted with 'the word spoken through angels' this is a summary of the final revelation. The inspired author knows that he just cannot describe this fully and he therefore writes 'so great a salvation', in order to give some idea of its incomparable greatness. He uses a similar expression in 'such a high priest' (8:1) and of course the 'salvation' and 'priest' are inseparably bound together because Jesus is the eternal Saviour.

Salvation is to be viewed against the background of sin and all its effects (1:3) and includes a restoration of the glory which existed before the Fall (2:5). It is found in Jesus, the incarnate Son (2:10) because he did all that was necessary to procure it (5:9). It is eternal, that is, heavenly and everlasting (7:25) and, when he comes again, all its benefits will be fully received by all who keep on believing (9:28 and 10:39).

Its several 'speakers'.

Although this salvation is so great that words cannot exhaustively describe it, it is made known by means of words, or in a message. Like the law, it too is capable of being spoken because it is God's wise plan (words convey thoughts), and it needs to be declared, since human beings are ignorant because of sin.

There are three messengers of salvation mentioned here, namely, the Lord Jesus, those who heard him (the apostles) and God himself. While they all speak about the same subject, something distinctive is said about each of them as messengers. Their combined testimony to the gospel is infinitely superior to that of angels to the law, even to countless myriads of them. We will consider each in turn.

i. *The Lord*

This is a reference to the Lord/Son who is about to be personally named as Jesus (verse 9). The focus is on his earthly ministry, a subject of considerable importance in this letter in relation to the message of salvation. He is said to have 'first' proclaimed salvation, not because no one before him had had anything to say about it (think, for example, of the prophets) but because he actualized it in time and space. Prior to him, there could only be prediction and after him, only attestation. Strictly speaking, he was the first gospel-preacher because his coming inaugurated 'the last days' and his death and resurrection accomplished redemption.

ii. *Those who heard him*

Those referred to here are not necessarily the apostles, but it is they who are primarily in view. The emphasis is on the fact that they had been 'hearers' of the Lord and so could guarantee to others the historicity of his teaching, deeds, and especially his resurrection which confirmed his identity as Lord and Saviour. This of course is what the apostles did (see *John* 15:27; *Acts* 1:21–22; 5;32; ; *2 Pet.* 1:16–18; *1 John* 1:1–3). They made known what they had seen and heard. Salvation is not an idea, myth or a theory. It is plain fact.

iii. *God himself*

While God was behind and present in his Son's speaking on earth, he also bore testimony to the report that those human preachers of the gospel gave. As they spoke he worked in ways that were calculated to draw people's attention to the message which they were making known, disclosing something of its nature – and not to the speakers themselves. *'Signs and wonders and miracles'* form a recurring triplet in the New Testament. The words are not always found in the same order, but each of them carries its own shade of meaning. The word *'signs'* points to the fact that *'wonders'* are not just eye-catching but have something to say to mind and conscience, and *'miracles'* indicates that these stupendous events are inexplicable on any other basis than that God is at work. Such interventions by God by way of an accompaniment to the preaching of the 'saving word' are not unlimited or haphazard. They are all 'according to His own will'.

3. THE EXHORTATION ENFORCED – HOW SHALL WE ESCAPE?

We have noted that there is an argument from the lesser to the greater in these verses with regard to the divine word, from law to salvation. This is also the case with regard to punishment or retribution, although that is not made explicit yet. Later on, the writer will speak of 'severer punishment' in 10:29. Here the emphasis is on certainty: the greater certainty of punishment implied in the question, ' If no sin was unpunished in the Old Testament, how can any be in the New?'

The New is not just a disclosure of the love of God. Much less does it contradict the emphasis of the Old on his justice and holiness. In fact, the New Testament is clearer and fuller on this than the Old Testament, as can be seen by looking at what Jesus, the incarnate Son of God, taught about Hell, over against the prophets, for example. God's justice will exact all that repudiation of his gospel merits. It certainly cannot be the case that a greater revelation from God will minimize the seriousness of a casual and superficial response to it. More light does mean more responsibility. Salvation from sin is a matter of life or death – eternally!

It ought to be underlined that the thrust of this warning is not directed to those who had never heard the gospel, and therefore never could profess to receive it. In their case punishment is no less certain, but it will not be as severe as it will be in the case of those who, having heard it and professed to receive it, then live carelessly.

4

Who Rules?

⁵ For He did not subject to angels the world to come, concerning which we are speaking. ⁶ But one has testified somewhere, saying, 'What is man, that Thou rememberest him? Or the son of man, that Thou art concerned about him? ⁷ Thou hast made him for a little while lower than the angels; Thou hast crowned him with glory and honor, and hast appointed him over the works of Thy hands; ⁸ Thou hast put all things in subjection under his feet.' For in subjecting all things to him, He left nothing that is not subject to him. But now we do not yet see all things subjected to him. ⁹ But we do see Him who has been made for a little while lower than the angels, namely Jesus, because of the suffering of death crowned with glory and honor, that by the grace of God He might taste death for every one. ¹⁰ For it was fitting for Him, for whom are all things, and through whom are all things, in bringing many sons to glory, to perfect the author of their salvation through sufferings. ¹¹ For both He who sanctifies and those who are sanctified are all from one Father; for which reason He is not ashamed to call them brethren, ¹² saying, 'I will proclaim Thy name to My brethren, in the midst of the congregation I will sing Thy praise.' ¹³ And again, 'I will put My trust in Him.' And again, 'Behold, I and the children whom God has given me.' ¹⁴ Since then the children share in flesh and blood, He Himself likewise also partook of the same, that through death He might render powerless him who had the power of death, that is, the devil; ¹⁵ and might deliver those who through fear of death were subject to slavery all their lives. ¹⁶ For assuredly He does not give help to angels, but He gives help to the seed of Abraham.

[17] Therefore, He had to be made like His brethren in all things, that He might become a merciful and faithful high priest in things pertaining to God, to make propitiation for the sins of the people. [18] For since He Himself was tempted in that which He has suffered, He is able to come to the aid of those who are tempted (Heb. 2:5–18).

The opening of this section of *Hebrews* contains the significant words, 'the world to come'. What do they mean? To understand them we must take our stand in the first century AD and look backwards in time from then and not forwards from our own day. We must think of how the Old Testament divided history, from the point of view of God's plan, into two ages. There was 'this age (or world)' which stood for the present and 'the world' or 'age to come' which was the age of the expected Messiah. The transition from the one to the other is referred to as 'the end of the ages' (see 9:26).

'The world to come' is therefore the final era of God's redemptive purpose. It corresponds to the 'last days' (see 1:2) which the author has been writing about and is still discussing, as is made clear by his use of the present tense, 'of which we are speaking', in verse 5. In the section before us he concentrates particularly on the administration of this age, or rather the identity of its ruler, speaking negatively before positively. We will consider each of these in turn.

Who Does Not Rule 'the World to Come'?

Angels

The meaning emerging from the Old Testament quotations in chapter 1 is that angels are servants and not rulers. The writer now asserts this unambiguously, declaring that angels do not rule because God has not assigned such authority to them. He is adamant on this point because those he addressed were giving angels a far higher place in the new era than actually belonged to them. By declaring that rule has not been assigned to them by God, the writer is also saying that they are not to be regarded in that way by any one. Contemporary interest in angels and 'the supernatural' should not be confused with authentic Christianity. Christians are therefore not to consult star-gazers or palm-readers.

Who Does Rule 'the World to Come'?

It is noteworthy that the writer does not immediately balance his negation with a positive identification of the ruler of this 'new world'. He first introduces a lengthy quotation from Psalm 8. Why does he do that? Is he not wandering from his point? No, of course not! His introduction of the Psalm text is deliberate on his part, and it is intimately related to his main theme. It all leads up to verse 9 where, in a very striking way, he names the ruler of this new world order. Let us follow his thinking.

Psalm 8 is generally thought of as a psalm about the created universe, and it obviously has such associations. But in the thinking of the inspired author, it is also relevant to 'the world to come'. It therefore speaks of two worlds, not one. It refers to the world of nature and to the world of grace and it refers to man as the ruler of both. Just as man was to rule, for God, the world he made, so he is to do with regard to the world which God is renewing. Just as it was not angels who ruled the earth, though they were exalted above mankind, so also, they do not rule the new world. Everything apart from God has been put under man's feet. It is man, therefore, who is to rule and not angels.

But while that has been determined, it is not visible – *not yet!* Man, God's appointed ruler, is not in control and the 'world' is not reverberating with the praise of God – but it will, and it will through Jesus. What is more, this is already under way because 'we see' Jesus. He has come and is visible to faith by the Spirit and we share in his reign.

This is the point in the letter where 'the Son' is first identified, and it is with a human not a divine name. The 'Son' of God is the man Jesus. He is therefore the second, or the last Adam, the forerunner, or pioneer ('author' in verse 10), and the representative head (verses 11–18) of a new mankind, which constitutes a family and a church, as verses 10–18 make clear. He has brothers whom he teaches to reign and to sing God's praise with and through him.

But let us follow the author's argument, keeping in mind the truth that it is man who rules 'the world to come'. The author's thinking has three steps or aspects to it. First, he speaks of *man as originally created,* secondly, of *the Son of God as incarnate,* and thirdly, of *the new humanity, as redeemed.*

1. *Man as originally created.*

There are two basic descriptions here of man as he was originally created by God. They are that he was *made lower than the angels*, but that he was *crowned with glory and honour, and appointed to rule over all created things*. We will consider each of these briefly;

i. *Made lower than the angels.*

The expression 'a little lower' implies the higher rank which angels possess as created spirit-beings. It is no part of the writer's thinking to deny them any of their proper dignity in the interests of the case that he is advocating. 'A little lower' can be translated 'a little while lower', and that is better because it suits both Adam as created and the 'Son' who becomes incarnate. Both were, in due time, exalted above the angels.

ii. *Crowned with glory and honour, and appointed over all other created things.*

Even though man is not as exalted as angels, but more limited, it is he, not they, who is made in the image and likeness of God. Angels are never said to be in God's image, but man is. He has the intellectual, moral and spiritual capacities to act as God's vice-regent on the earth. A dignity has been conferred upon him. He is given the sacred duty of ruling for God over all created things.

2. *The Son of God as Incarnate*

The divine mandate which was given to Adam and Eve (*Gen.* 1:26–28) has never been fully realized by any human being. Man is superior to all that is earthly, strives for control over it and yet falls back defeated, time and again. The evidence is undeniable, in every sphere of life. Man is not ruling. He is 'free, yet everywhere in chains'. This is because all things are no longer under him, as they once were. Something has happened to disturb that original harmony. It is Adam's sin. But God's word has not been rescinded and cannot fail. It therefore awaits fulfilment. And so the writer says in verse 8, 'we do not yet see all things subjected to him'.

This second step relates to the Son who became man, without ceasing to be what he was. What is in view at this point is what was necessary to restore the harmony which human sin had disrupted and shattered irreparably from a human point of view. Adam, God's created son (*Gen.* 5:1-3 and *Luke* 3:38) had ruined the world of nature; Jesus, God's incarnate Son restores it. And how does he do that? It is by 'the suffering of death'. The recovery of man's dominion and human harmony lost through sin is only possible by undergoing the penalty of that sin, which is death. Jesus did not come to try to make this world a better place but to make a new world, a new heaven and a new earth, and this he did by dying. There is no 'social gospel'; there will be no Utopia, no way back to Eden.

The name 'Jesus' is especially appropriate to this grand scheme, and the writer introduces it at this point with effect. Perhaps he has also held it back because he knew that those whom he addressed were ill at ease with the reality of the humanity of Jesus and especially with the fact that he suffered. So he spoke first about the Son, as Lord and God – designations which are connected with the heavenly world before identifying him with Jesus.

3. *The New Humanity as Redeemed*
So the original pattern not only highlights human failure but points to its fulfilment in another man, namely Jesus, and in others because of him. Jesus, the Son of God, not only becomes an individual member of the human race by his incarnation but also the progenitor of a new human race by acting as its representative. The term 'man' is generic. It is equivalent to 'human'. These verses describe those who comprise the new humanity and how they are joined to Jesus so as to benefit from all he did.

i. *What is said about them?*
They are described as follows: 'every one' (verse 9); 'many sons' (verse 10); 'all from one' and 'brethren' (verse 11); 'children' (verse 13); those who 'share in flesh and blood' (verse 14); those who are 'subject to slavery through fear of death' (verse 15); 'the seed of Abraham' (verse 16) and '[the] tempted' (verse 18).

Now, all these descriptions do not apply to every single person universally, though some do, for example the fact that all have flesh and blood and are characterized by fear of death and bondage to sin. All of them do hold good, however, with regard to Christians, and them alone. Viewed as a company, they do not form a small group. They are 'many' in number and in diversity, but every one of them is special because Jesus died for each of them.

These epithets listed can be categorized in terms of what people were by nature, what they are by grace, and what they still are although they have received grace. By nature, they have a flesh-and-blood existence and their life is characterized by fear of death and bondage. By grace, they are the seed of Abraham, and as such are sons of God by adoption, brothers of Jesus Christ, and children of a heavenly Father, although, partaking of flesh and blood, they are still tempted.

ii. *How are they joined to their new head?*

There are two complementary emphases in these verses that provide an answer to this question. The first is that they are united to Christ because God chose them in love and gave them to him, as verse 13 makes clear. This was done in eternity, before time began. Then verse 16 speaks of the Son's grasping or taking hold of those thus given to him. This refers to what happens in time, as he makes himself their high priest by living and dying for them, and then as he calls them to himself by the gospel.

PART 2

Jesus the Apostle
and High Priest
(3:1 – 10:18)

Having shown Jesus' unique lordship in God's self-revealing and all-restoring purpose, the writer narrows down his lens to focus on his apostleship and high priesthood. These are the ministries of the Messiah on which he concentrates in the rest of his letter. Just as Moses, and Joshua after him, were to lead the children of Israel out of Egypt, through the wilderness, and to the Promised Land, and Aaron and his descendants were to intercede for them on their way, so Jesus leads his people out of the kingdom of darkness, through this wilderness of a world, praying for them on their way to their heavenly home.

5

The Household of God

*Therefore, holy brethren, partakers of a heavenly calling,
consider Jesus, the Apostle and High Priest of our confession.
² He was faithful to Him who appointed Him, as Moses also
was in all His house. ³ For He has been counted worthy of more
glory than Moses, by just so much as the builder of the house
has more honor than the house. ⁴ For every house is built by
someone, but the builder of all things is God. ⁵ Now Moses was
faithful in all His house as a servant, for a testimony of
those things which were to be spoken later; ⁶ but Christ was
faithful as a Son over His house whose house we are, if we hold
fast our confidence and the boast of our hope firm until the end*
(Heb. 3:1–6).

'Apostle' and 'house' are the two key words in the teaching of
this section and we begin with a study of each in turn.

The Apostle

This is the only place in the New Testament where the word
'apostle' is used specifically of Jesus. However, the verb 'to send' is
often used of him, and by him of himself (for example in John
10:36). The noun is generally used of others who were either sent
by Jesus personally, namely the 'twelve apostles' (*Matt.* 10:2), or by
the churches (*Acts* 14:4; *2 Cor.* 8:23).

The important thing to discover whenever the word 'apostle' is
used in the New Testament is the identity of 'the sender' and the
nature of the mission on which 'the apostle' is sent. This is because
an apostle went on his task with the authority of the sender and
with the gifts necessary for the assignment. The Jewish Sanhedrin
had its apostles and Saul of Tarsus was one of them (see *Acts*

9:1–2). So there is an appropriate use for the term 'apostle' today. However, it probably clarifies matters to use the term 'church-messenger' or 'missionary' so that the absolute uniqueness of that group of men whom Jesus personally chose and sent to found the church on himself might be safeguarded. Jesus and Moses (and to a lesser extent Joshua, see *Heb.* 4:8) were 'apostles' because they were each sent by God to govern and guide his people.

THE HOUSE

This term is closely connected with the word 'apostle' in these verses and it is used six times there. It can mean 'household' or 'family' as well as 'a building' and it is perhaps used in both senses in these verses. In the first part of verse 4 it probably means a building; in verse 6 it must mean 'people'. In the Old Testament we often find the expression 'the house of Israel'. This is echoed, or fulfilled in 10:21 where we read of 'the house of God', that is the people of God related to him through the Messiah.

What is taught in these verses can be set out under three headings: one people (house), its two forms (apostles), but its one and only founder.

1. *One People*

Apart from verse 4, where the word 'house' might refer to a building, and so to the general truth that everything constructed has a builder, it refers to people. In these verses there is only one 'house' referred to and so there is only one people. Moses, Christ, and all who believe in Jesus, are in this house. There is therefore a solid unity that characterizes the people of God across the different phases of God's redemptive self-revelation.This is a basic strand of the teaching of this letter and it is made explicit in 11:39–40. It is, of course, the fundamental assertion of Romans 11:12–36.

2. *Two Forms, corresponding to Two Apostles*

God's 'house' was, as it were, built in two stages, corresponding to the 'apostolic' ministries first of Moses and then of Jesus. Each of these was appointed by God to minister in his house, and each was faithful in the task assigned to him (verses 2, 5–6). But in spite of this harmony there are some differences between their respective ministries that must be noted.

i. *Differences between Moses and Jesus*

Moses was God's 'servant'. The noun which is used here is neither the word for 'slave', nor that for 'deacon', both of which occur frequently in the New Testament. The term used indicates *service of a deity* and occurs nowhere else in the New Testament. It points to the fact that Moses occupied a dignified, not a menial, place in God's service. Moses was a prophet (*Num.* 12:7–8); a priest (*Exod.* 24:8) and a king (*Deut.* 33:5). Galatians 3:19 designates him as a 'mediator' of a covenant, and this is borne out later in Hebrews 10:19. The 'church in the wilderness' (see *Acts* 7:37–38 and *Heb.* 3:7–4:13) was placed by God under the 'apostleship' of Moses (see *1 Cor.* 10:2).

The fact that Jesus was also an 'apostle' appointed by God carries with it the idea of service, but he is not termed a 'servant', not even by the use of the distinguished word used of Moses. He is an 'apostle'; but even more than that. Verse 6 says that Jesus is the 'Christ' of God, and 'Son' of God. His mediatorial sonship, as expressed in the previous two chapters, is in view here. He is therefore *over* the house and not merely *in* it.

ii. *Differences between their Ministries*

Verse 5b relates the ministry of Moses to that of Jesus in terms of 'a testimony . . . of things [to] be spoken later'. This is a most important statement. It indicates that the one thing was not only preliminary to the other, but predictive of it. What Moses dealt with pointed forward to what was going to be revealed in Christ. There is therefore this basic harmony between the two stages of messianic 'house-building', just as there is between the two eras of revelation, as the opening statements of the letter make clear. (Three other expressions which are important for an understanding of the relationship between the old and the new are found in 8:5a and 9:9 and we will consider them later.)

3. *Only One Founder*

'To build a house' and 'to found a family' are translations of the same Hebrew phrase (see *Exod.* 1:21). Verse 4 says that it is God who builds all things. Every significant arrangement in the church is therefore of his appointing, as was everything in the Tabernacle too. But verse 3 attributes the 'building' of this one people of God specifically to Jesus. This points to the fact that, just as the universe was brought into being by God through Jesus, so it is with his one redeemed people. It is because Jesus is *Christ*, that is, God's messianic Son that a church is possible. 1 Chronicles 17:11–12 and Zechariah 6:12–13 predict that it is the son of David who will build the house, that is, the temple of God, which is, of course, his people.

'WHOSE HOUSE WE ARE'.

The writer now emphasizes that the people he is addressing belong, along with himself, to Christ and not to Moses. He describes them from two complementary angles in these verses. Verse 1 refers to the confession of faith that they have made. Verse 6 refers to the need to continue in it, with certainty and gladness.

1. *Their Confession*

The verb 'to confess', which is widely used in the New Testament, refers to the making of a formal, public declaration. However, the fact that half of the six New Testament occurrences of the noun 'confession' are found in this epistle (see also 4:14 and 10:23) is an indication of its importance to the message of this writer. As their confession qualified them to be regarded and treated as Christians, so it provided him with a basis for his exhortation to them.

In the Gospels, Jesus required public confession of his would-be followers and the apostle Paul explained its significance in Romans.10:9–11. Often, to confess Christ publicly led to judicial proceedings being taken, either in the Jewish synagogue (*John* 9:22) or a Gentile law-court. This is because an explicit statement, 'Jesus is Lord' (*1 Cor.* 12: 3), carried the implicit denial of the existence of all other 'so-called lords and gods' (*1 Cor.* 8:5–6). These Hebrews had made such a confession.

What we are told in 3:1 about their profession of faith contains nothing about their experiences, but that dimension is mentioned later (see 10:32), so that making a confession is not just accepting a creed. What is emphasized here relates entirely to the one whom they acknowledged. They had recognized Jesus of Nazareth as the divinely-appointed and long-awaited Messiah and had acknowledged him as apostle and high priest. They had professed to submit to his authority as the one sent from God to lead them, and to trust in his atoning ministry which admitted him into the presence of God for them. This was a new religion.

Professing faith in Christ entitled them to be regarded as *'holy brethren and partakers of the heavenly calling'*. Implicit in the former is, of course, their fraternal relationship to each other, whether male or female. But it is as those who are 'holy', that is those who have been separated from the world to God through Christ's death and by the Spirit, that they are related to each other. The distinctiveness of the church is emphasized in this description, as well as its domestic character, and neither of these is to be emphasized at the expense of the other.

Similarly, while the church is an earthly society, it is made up of those who have received a *heavenly calling,* that is, a call which is both *from* and *to* heaven. God's own voice has sounded in their hearts through the preaching of the gospel and, willingly and gladly, they have responded to it (see *2 Thess.* 2:12–14). This refers to their pilgrim status and character. 'Heavenly' is an important term in this letter, as we shall see.

2. *Their Continuance*

Because the writer is dealing with his readers on the basis of their profession of faith, he can exhort them to prove its genuineness or sincerity by continuing to look forward in hope. Faith and hope are inseparably connected, as the opening verse of Chapter 11 makes clear. This is the area of their need, as is shown in 3:14; 5:11; 10:23; and the whole of 11 and 12. Their hope was waning, and so their faith was shaking, or was it the other way round? Faith has an *object* and hope has a *prospect* and both are wrapped up in the same person, Jesus Christ who, as apostle and high priest, promises and provides more than his people have as yet received. Not to continue in hope is therefore to cast doubt upon the reality of one's faith, but, more seriously, upon Christ's honour and faithfulness.

3. *Their 'Consideration'*

But how are they going to continue? What is available to help them? The answer to these related questions is bound up in the words 'consider Jesus'. This is an obligation, but one which should be in no way burdensome to them. There are no easy, instant solutions to the challenges and difficulties of living as a Christian in a fallen world. Duties done rightly, that is, out of love and in faith, are the means by which divine aid is graciously given.

The duty which helps one to hold on in faith and joy is expressed in a call to 'consider' – an English word which no longer has the force which once it did. It does not mean to give occasional mental acknowledgment to a fact, not even to the fact that Jesus is 'apostle and high priest', but to concentrate the mind on the reality and rich significance of this truth. The result will be an increasing, not diminishing, faith and hope in the apostle and high priest.

6

On Pilgrimage

[7] *Therefore just as the Holy Spirit says, 'Today if you hear His voice, [8] do not harden your hearts as when they provoked Me, as in the day of trial in the wilderness, [9] where your fathers tried Me by testing Me, and saw My works for forty years. [10] Therefore I was angry with this generation, and said, "They always go astray in their heart; and they did not know My ways"; [11] As I swore in My wrath, "They shall not enter My rest." ' [12] Take care, brethren, lest there should be in any one of you an evil, unbelieving heart, in falling away from the living God. [13] But encourage one another day after day, as long as it is still called 'Today', lest any one of you be hardened by the deceitfulness of sin. [14] For we have become partakers of Christ, if we hold fast the beginning of our assurance firm until the end; [15] while it is said, 'Today if you hear His voice, do not harden your hearts, as when they provoked Me.' [16] For who provoked Him when they had heard? Indeed, did not all those who came out of Egypt led by Moses? [17] And with whom was He angry for forty years? Was it not with those who sinned, whose bodies fell in the wilderness? [18] And to whom did He swear that they should not enter His rest, but to those who were disobedient? [19] And so we see that they were not able to enter because of unbelief.*

[1] Therefore, let us fear lest, while a promise remains of entering His rest, any one of you should seem to have come short of it. [2] For indeed we have had good news preached to us, just as they also; but the word they heard did not profit them, because it was not united by faith in those who heard. [3] For we

who have believed enter that rest; just as He has said, 'As I swore in My wrath, they shall not enter My rest,' although His works were finished from the foundation of the world. ⁴ For He has thus said somewhere concerning the seventh day, 'And God rested on the seventh day from all His works', ⁵ and again in this passage, 'They shall not enter My rest.' ⁶ Since therefore it remains for some to enter it, and those who formerly had good news preached to them failed to enter because of disobedience, ⁷ He again fixes a certain day, 'Today,' saying through David after so long a time just as has been said before, 'Today if you hear His voice, do not harden your hearts.' ⁸ For if Joshua had given them rest, He would not have spoken of another day after that. ⁹ There remains therefore a Sabbath rest for the people of God. ¹⁰ For the one who has entered His rest has himself also rested from his works, as God did from His. ¹¹ Let us therefore be diligent to enter that rest, lest anyone fall through following the same example of disobedience. ¹² For the word of God is living and active and sharper than any two-edged sword, and piercing as far as the division of soul and spirit, of both joints and marrow, and able to judge the thoughts and intentions of the heart. ¹³ And there is no creature hidden from His sight, but all things are open and laid bare to the eyes of Him with whom we have to do (Heb. 3:7–4:13).

These verses should be read as a unit, ignoring the chapter division that comes after verse 19. When that is done, the fact that Psalm 95 runs like a refrain throughout the passage becomes obvious. This Psalm is referred to in nineteen of the twenty-nine verses in this section, and it is quoted five times. Obviously, the writer wanted to stress something to his readers. What was it? It was that they were in 'a wilderness situation', and God was speaking to them the same message as he had to their forefathers. How were they going to respond? He has just reminded them (3:6) about the need to persevere to 'the end'. They are not there yet. Like others before them, and all believers after them, they are in a wilderness; that is, they are on pilgrimage to that 'better country' which is 'a heavenly one' (see 11:16). We will examine this section by following the writer's lines of thought as he uses Psalm 95.

The Scope of Psalm 95

Obviously, the writer believes that this Psalm is most suitable as a basis for what he has to say. Two reasons for this are evident. First, there is a threefold scope of reference in the Psalm itself; and secondly, its theme is 'rest'. Taking the time of the Psalm's composition as the fixed point, he shows that it looked backwards and forwards. We will therefore consider how the reference of the Psalm is to the past (retrospective), the present (contemporary), and the future (prospective).

i. *Retrospective*

Psalm 95 speaks of 'the day of trial in the wilderness', and our writer quotes at length from it in 3:7–12. The incident in view is recorded in Numbers 14. On the border of the Promised Land, and after all that God had done for them throughout forty years, the unbelief of the people reached its climax. God then declared on oath (*Num.* 14: 28) that none over twenty years of age, except Caleb and Joshua, would enter the land. This took place around 1400 BC.

ii. *Contemporary*

In 4:7 we have the words, 'saying through David after so long a time'. This refers to the period some 400 years later when the Psalm was actually composed by King David, the sweet singer of Israel. Although the people were now in the land that had been promised to them, God was reminding them of the past.

iii. *Prospective*

This includes the period between David and the writing of this epistle and even beyond that. It is the word 'Today', and who originally spoke that word, which justifies this conclusion. The real speaker was not David but the Holy Spirit (verse 7), and so the appropriate verb tense is 'says' not 'said'. The word 'Today' in the Psalm was not only intended to refer to Moses' day or Joshua's day (4:8) or David's day but to God's 'today', that is, the 'day' in which he calls people into his rest. This supra-temporal reference leads up to the statement that 'the word of God is living' in 4:12 because, although spoken at a particular time and recorded later, it transcends time and speaks of eternity.

THE THEME OF THE PSALM

This is *God's rest*. It is referred to ten times in this passage, and is God's good news to man. It is the 'gospel' (4:2) and is depicted by the sabbath-rest that followed the completion of God's creative activity (4:4). Into that rest with God, Adam and Eve entered before ever they began to serve their Lord and King. But it was forfeited by their sin which turned their work into toil and life into death. But the rest remained as a promise through the predicted seed of the woman, and just as expulsion from Eden did not destroy it, so occupation of the land of promise did not fulfil it.

The 'sabbath rest' is fellowship with God which is entered into on earth by faith (4:3), and yet is still to be entered (4:11). It is both present and future, but not in equal measure. The best is yet to be, and those addressed were to press on to enter it fully, as were those in Old Testament times, whether they were in the land or not. The fact that, in the Old Testament, the seventh day is connected not only with creation but also with redemption provides the basis for it to be changed in New Testament times, and for the first day to be kept as holy to the Lord.

THE PURPOSE OF ITS USE

As has been said, the writer wants those he is addressing to realize that they are in a wilderness situation. The Bible nowhere overlooks, let alone denies, the reality of the earthly existence of the people of God. Although it emphasizes and exults in the fact that those who belong to the household of Jesus Christ possess a heavenly life and destiny, it makes clear that they are not yet in the full possession of all that is prepared for them. They are already part of a great company that transcends time, space and even death (see 12:22–4), but they are not yet in the 'city which has foundations whose builder and maker is God' (11:10). They are therefore 'strangers and pilgrims' in this world.

The writer wants the Hebrews to visualize themselves as being in the wilderness with God's rest before them. He wants them to realize the danger that faces them, but to know the way to respond to it. He therefore warns and encourages them. This is his regular mode of address, warning *and* encouragement, usually in that order. In particular, he wants his readers to avoid the repetition of their forefathers' unbelief and to appropriate the reality of the rest of which the Psalm speaks.

i. *Avoid a repetition*

In chapter 4:11 the writer speaks of 'the same example of disobedience'. He uses two words in this section to describe the unworthy reaction of the wilderness generation, namely *unbelief* and *disobedience*. There is an important distinction in meaning between them. Both relate to the Word of God as declared. The one, unbelief, does not receive God's Word; the other, disobedience, acts in opposition to it. The former leads to the latter. Both are seen in the account in Numbers 14, unbelief in verses 1–38 and disobedience in verses 39–45.

How can this be avoided? The answer is given in negative and positive terms in 3:12–13. Negatively, a condition of heart is warned against which will result in a fateful step being taken. A heart which is evil and unbelieving is an unregenerate heart and, even though someone has made a public profession of Jesus Christ, he or she may be unregenerate. Profession does not always mean possession. This warning is more specific than 'drifting' and 'neglecting' in 2:1,3 and it anticipates the fatal step referred to in 6:6 and 10: 29. But even so the writer addresses this warning to those he calls 'brothers'. He does not cast a doubt on their profession because such a possibility exists. Christians are to take heed to their hearts (*Prov.* 4: 23).

Positively, a course of action is to be followed daily. Introspection is therefore to be avoided. Self-examination is one thing but self-preoccupation is another. What is more this activity has regard to others as well as oneself. We are not only to 'pull up our own socks' but to 'help others to their feet'. The best way to counteract both the pull and pall of sin is by persevering in partaking of Christ in confidence (verse 14).

ii. *Appropriate the Reality*

The way to do this is found in 4:1–2 and 11. It is by continuing to believe that the danger of 'falling short' or 'not entering in' is effectively countered. This is not because of any virtue or merit which resides in believing, but because rest is freely promised to those who believe. The kind of faith that has this effect is one that is based on the promise (verse 2) and is characterized by 'fear [and] diligence'. This is not a fear which is characterized by either doubt or terror. It is a reverential, sobering realization that others have fallen, that we are weak, and that we have a foe and must persevere in obeying God (see *2 Cor.* 11:3; 12:20,21; and 7:11).

But what is said about the Word of God in 4:12–13 includes God's promise of rest as well as his commands about how to enter it. He stands by and upholds, not only his commands, but also his promises. His promise of rest (4:1) is therefore not to be trifled with but trusted – wholeheartedly and ongoingly. He is just as concerned that his promise is not believed as he is that his commands are not obeyed – perhaps more so, because his promise expresses his grace and kindness. He therefore swears an oath that the unbelieving and disobedient will not be allowed to enter his rest, and his anger or wrath will be poured out on them. And who dares dispute the propriety of that?

7

A Throne of Grace

¹⁴ Since then we have a great high priest who has passed through the heavens, Jesus the Son of God, let us hold fast our confession. ¹⁵ For we do not have a high priest who cannot sympathize with our weaknesses, but one who has been tempted in all things as we are, yet without sin. ¹⁶ Let us therefore draw near with confidence to the throne of grace, that we may receive mercy and may find grace to help in time of need (Heb. 4: 14–16).

The priestly status and ministry of the Lord Jesus Christ is the theme of this section, and it is what distinguishes *Hebrews* from all other New Testament writings. Having alluded to it in 1:3; 2:17–18 and 3:1 the writer now begins to give it detailed consideration. Following his pattern of comparing and contrasting Jesus with figures of Old Testament revelation, he presents the uniqueness of Jesus as high priest in relation to Aaron and to Melchizedek. This is done in the chapters that follow. But first, he presents Jesus as high priest in terms that are full of encouragement.

The few verses in the section before us contain a call to action, but also give a reason on which that call is based. They therefore combine exhortation and encouragement. This connection between duty and doctrine is of the essence of authentic preaching, although the order in which they are presented may vary from one sermon to another. Truly Christian activity is neither mind-less nor motive-less behaviour. It is related to gospel privilege and obligation because it is in the nature of believing obedience to God's truth, his promise and his precept.

Those addressed are in a 'time of need'. What this was may be gathered from the fact that they have been told to be 'diligent to enter the rest' (see 4:11), and to 'hold fast their profession' (3:6,14). They were in a crisis over faith and obedience. Would they keep on believing and obeying or . . . ? To encourage them to persevere the writer reminds them that they and he (for he was aware that he needed to persevere as well) had a great high priest who could, and would, provide help for all who came to him for it.

WHAT THEY HAD – A 'GREAT' HIGH PRIEST

From the fact that the writer repeatedly uses some form of the verb 'to have' (see 6:19; 8:1; 10:19–22, 34; 13:10, 14) it is possible to deduce that those addressed were forgetful of their privileges. Perhaps they had a 'have-not' mentality because, for them, a rather plain Christianity compared so unfavourably with Judaism and all its trappings. This was particularly true with regard to a high priest – they had one when they were practising Jews, as their fellow-nationals around them still did, but that was so no longer.

The preacher not only flatly contradicts such thinking by his use of the participle 'having', but he also turns their thinking on its head by adding the adjective 'great' to qualify 'high priest'. He is therefore not only asserting that they *do* have a high priest, but he is saying that the one they have is infinitely better than the one the Jews possess. In the Old Testament era one priest was differentiated for life from all others and called a 'high' or 'great' priest. But the writer here uses both adjectives to indicate that their high priest was far superior to all Jewish high priests.

What then is 'great' about Jesus as 'high priest'? There are two general points made in these verses. The first relates to his supremacy and the second to his sympathy and each is in its own way as great as the other.

i. *Supremacy of the Highest Possible Order*

There are two aspects to this supremacy. The first is that Jesus 'has passed through the heavens'. This is why he is no longer visible. The writer will show later (see 9:24) that the most which all other priests could do was to go behind a man-made curtain into the holiest place, one which was itself constructed out of earthly materials. Jesus has gone beyond 'the heavens', that is, all that is external to God and is actually 'in the presence of God' for his people and is 'at the right hand of the throne' (see 8:1). This means that he is the executor of God's purposes towards his people. Secondly, he is 'the Son of God'. His indestructible deity (see 7:16) provides the foundation both for his work of atonement in human flesh and for his intercession in heaven. He reigns and distributes blessings.

Given these, it should be quite superfluous to say that Jesus is a 'great' high priest but, sad to say, and not only then but also today, he needs to be differentiated from every other priest, whether past, present or future. No one ranks alongside him in the estimate of God, and therefore no one should be bracketed with him in the estimate of Christian people.

ii. *Sympathy to the Greatest Possible Degree*

Having doubled an adjective in order to make a point emphatically, the writer now doubles a negative – 'we do not have one who cannot'. This means, of course, 'we do have one who can'. But why put it in the negative? He does so in order to stress that his supremacy does not diminish his sympathy and that, it seems, is what those addressed needed to realize. The high priest they had was not only one who could not have been higher for them, but one who could not be nearer to them as well! How favoured they were, and we are!

Our high priest could not be closer, either to God or to us. We do not need his earthly mother to represent us to him, or anyone else! Perish the thought! The one who was (and is) the divine Son in heaven, not only has been on earth but still remembers what it was like to be here below and it is as such that he ministers to and for his people. Not only is he not aloof, he is more than even a concerned onlooker. As one who experienced infirmity and adversity his concern is more than empathy. It is true compassion; he feels for and suffers with his needy people. He was 'tempted' in infirmity and 'triumphant' in it. (These are explained in 5:7–9.) He knew need, but he did not sin. The Hebrews thought they were alone, but they were not. Nor are we.

WHAT THEY COULD HAVE – HELP

Confidence was what they lacked, and that is the key to true perseverance (see 3:6, 14; 6:11). Of course, this is not a confidence in oneself or in others like oneself, but a confidence in Christ, the great high priest, and in his ready aid to uphold his people so that they can hold on to faith and hope. The writer wants them to be sure that they can ask for such help – even though their weakness was partly the result of their sinful indolence. They were not to be hesitant with regard either to their profession of faith or to their approach to God. They were to come boldly to him, just as they were to stand boldly for him.

To be an object of mercy means that one is in a defenceless and pathetic condition. When people ask for mercy, their resources are non-existent and their only hope lies in evoking someone's pity. This is usually done in the language of pleading. But our high priest is already moved with pity towards his people before they come to him to ask for it. His mercies are 'tender', which means that he does not show mercy with a grudge. He delights to be merciful, time and time again.

But while merciful kindness is wonderful, more is needed. We need strength, and it is available. Remembering his own times of need on earth and how he was comforted and strengthened by his heavenly Father and ministering angels (see *Mark* 1:13 and *Luke* 22:43), he gives aid to his people when they are tempted and tested. His people should not therefore allow their weakness to disqualify them in their own minds from coming to him. Rather the reverse! He understands and will meet their need not only fully but also freely. His mercy cradles them and his might sets them on their feet.

8

Our High Priest

For every high priest taken from among men is appointed on behalf of men in things pertaining to God in order to offer both gifts and sacrifices for sins; ² he can deal gently with the ignorant and misguided, since he himself also is beset with weakness; ³ and because of it he is obligated to offer sacrifices for sins, as for the people, so also for himself. ⁴ And no one takes the honor to himself, but receives it when he is called by God, even as Aaron was. ⁵ So also Christ did not glorify Himself so as to become a high priest, but He who said to Him, 'Thou art My Son, today I have begotten Thee'; ⁶ just as He says also in another passage, 'Thou art a priest forever according to the order of Melchizedek.' ⁷ In the days of His flesh, when He offered up both prayers and supplications with loud crying and tears to Him who was able to save Him from death, and who was heard because of His piety, ⁸ although He was a Son, He learned obedience from the things which He suffered; ⁹ and having been made perfect, He became to all those who obey Him the source of eternal salvation; ¹⁰ being designated by God as a high priest according to the order of Melchizedek (Heb. 5:1–10).

At the heart of the encouraging exhortation the writer has just given is the emphasis that the high priest sympathizes with his people in every 'time of need'. In this section he concentrates further on the 'greatness' of his compassion by way of contrast with Aaron. He focuses first on Aaron (verses 1–4) and secondly on the Son (verses 5–10). The turning point is marked by the words 'so also Christ' at the beginning of verse 5. There is therefore a similarity between Aaron (and his successors) and Jesus in this matter of sympathy, but we shall see that there was also an all-important difference.

THE HUMANITY OF AARON (verses 1–4)

The necessity of a divine appointment for priestly ministry, which has already been mentioned (3:2), is found again in verses 1 and 4 of this passage. It is implied in the passive participle 'taken' in verse 1 which points to the action of God, and it is stated emphatically in verse 4 by means of a negation. Exodus 28–29 and Leviticus 8–9 record the institution of the Aaronic priesthood. This means that no high priest was to be installed as a result of his volunteering or being democratically elected. Korah, Dathan and Abiram (*Num.* 16) and king Uzziah (*2 Chron.*26:16–23) all bear witness, on the one hand, to the human tendency to intrude where one ought not, and, on the other, to the divine jealousy with which God upheld his sanctions.

However the main emphasis in this passage is on the merciful and gracious logic behind this divine arrangement. It was to encourage the needy to come to God. The high priest was 'taken from among men', not angels. Taking one of their own kind was intended to display two things: first, that there was a way for sinners to approach God via gifts and sacrifices, and secondly, since the high priest dealt with them in a gentle manner, that God would do so too. Aaron and his descendants were 'beset with weakness'. They were also sinners themselves and were not exempt from needing to offer sacrifice. As such, infirm and yet appointed by God, they were fitted to deal with 'the ignorant and erring' in the way in which God would have them dealt with – 'gently'.

The 'ignorant and erring' is a description of those who had sinned ignorantly or unwittingly and consequently strayed from the precepts of God. These sins included all those acts that contravened what was commanded and for which sacrifices were provided. It did not include capital offences or sinning deliberately or wilfully, as in 10:26.

The 'sympathy' which Aaron and his descendants were expected to show to worshippers arose out of an awareness of his own infirmity and, by all the laws, that is what should uniformly have happened. But there is a hint in the word translated 'can deal gently' in verse 4 that it would never be easy to express and that it could not be guaranteed. The word in question is not used anywhere else in the New Testament. It is a combination of two words, one meaning 'to feel or suffer', and the other (which gives us our word 'metre') having to do with measuring or moderating. It means to control instinctive feelings of impatience, or worse, in order to exhibit the infinite patience of God. All censoriousness, coldness or harshness on his part was to be concealed so that the needy worshipper might have a display of a God who was glad that he had come and even come again – and to 'seventy times seven' (*Matt.* 18:22). How this contrasts with what is displayed in 1 Samuel 2:12–17 and Jeremiah 5:31!

THE HUMANITY OF JESUS (verses 5–10)

Because Aaron and his descendants were so weak, it should have been no hard task for them to be sympathetic to sinful worshippers. But how could the divine Son, who was neither weak nor sinful, become sympathetic to such, and so become the kind of high priest which sinners need?

The answer is provided in the verses that follow. Verses 5 and 6 make clear that this was not achieved by the fiat of a divine appointment – even though his priesthood was superior to that of Aaron because it combined kingly rule with priestly intercession. (More will be said on this in commenting on chapter 7.) But it is not exaltation that leads to sympathy; rather it is humiliation.

The clauses in these verses which describe the humiliation of the Son are unique in Scripture. There is no parallel to them even in the sacred Gospel records. Yet, the opening words of verse 8, 'although he was a Son', make it clear that the contrast between deity and humanity which is so staggeringly portrayed in these verses should not be reduced by any minimizing of the Son's full deity. The unity of the God-Man is not only mysterious; it is essential for the salvation of sinners.

But even deity was not sufficient to make the Son all that sinners needed in a high priest. He had to become human and be perfected (verse 9), and verses 7 and 8 describe what was involved in this: He learned obedience. He became 'a disciple' and so became the procuring cause or 'source' (NASB) of eternal salvation.

To gather this profound material under some headings so as to promote meditation on it, we will ask and answer three questions in connection with the real learning process of which it speaks. They are as follows:

i. *What did the Son learn?*

The answer to this is quite clear. It was obedience. To understand this it is vital to distinguish in our minds between learning and knowledge. That difference is similar to the distinction between knowledge and wisdom. Wisdom is putting information into practice. It is being a disciple. Learning involves living.

The Son knew many things which ordinary human beings did not, and could not, know. Being the Son, he knew what was in man (*John* 2:25); and who he was, where he had come from and where he was going to (*John* 13:1–3). What is more, he knew why he had come into the world. What more then could he learn? Only what was involved in the actual doing of his Father's will; not in saying that he would do it, but doing that which from all eternity he had said he would. What a lesson!

ii. *When did he learn this?*

The answer to this is also quite clear. It was 'in the days of his flesh'. This expression refers to the period of his life on earth that was governed by his physical condition. It was from his birth to his death. For the Son to consent to the Father's will in eternity involved submission of a sort, but that can hardly be compared with his doing what he said he would, having personally entered a fallen world and having taken to himself an infirm body. His incarnation brought him within the limitations of time and space, the emotional and physical frailties of mind and body – and the actual reach of sinners and Satan. What a school!

iii. *How did he learn this?*

It was 'by the things that he suffered'. Obedience to God is never easy in a fallen world and in an infirm body – not even for a sinless person. To pray all night instead of sleeping, to go without food for forty days, was not easy. Suffering weakness and experiencing adversity was a new experience for the divine Son. Although it was not unanticipated by him, it could never have been experienced by him prior to Bethlehem. Such sufferings characterized the whole of his life from womb to tomb, and they became acute and intense, beyond human measurement or computation, as he neared the completion of the lesson in the school of suffering.

The event which is selected as the proof and manifestation of all this is the Son's experience in the Garden of Gethsemane. That must be what lies behind the details in verse 7. Although the Gospel writers do not refer to our Lord as weeping in the Garden, what they say is in keeping with this verse. When Jesus wept before, it was on account of others, but here he wept for himself. He was in need as he faced a cup extended to him by his Father which he knew contained all that sin merited at the bar of divine justice. His most awful suffering was that which coincided with the greatest demand made of him. Here the presentiment of it caused intense anguish to him – and he was sinless! What will bearing that wrath endlessly mean for the impenitent?

Being obedient to all his Father's will made his work complete, and it made him replete with the sympathy and the grace to help that his people need. Even now in heaven he still remembers his 'time of need', how he prayed in godly fear and was heard and helped, and so he will help all those who come to him in their time of need. As he was kept in death and raised from the dead, so will his people be, by his grace.

The Parenthesis
(5:11 – 6:20)

The similarity between the words of chapters 5:10 and 6:20 shows that the intervening section is a parenthesis. The writer postpones his intention of treating the glories of the priestly status and ministry of the Lord Jesus because he knows that the spiritual condition of those addressed would hinder them from understanding and appreciating what he has to say. This shows that the proclamation of God's truth is always to be for the benefit of the Lord's people and not for the display of the preacher's knowledge. It also indicates that the Lord's people can hinder the presentation of God's truth, and that when preaching is not understood and appreciated it is not always the fault of the preachers!

This whole passage is therefore an example of searching and kindly pastoral care. It is a mine of pastoral theology and we do well to remember that, because it is better known for the warning which it contains – the most awesome warning in the whole of the New Testament (6:4–8). Sadly, it is often forgotten that the most sublime comfort and assurance is included in it as well (6:18–20), and that the writer directed the words of warning and the words of comfort to the same group of people!

Being able to come to terms with this striking fact is therefore a test of the correctness of any interpretation of the text, because the inspired author could not contradict himself. To find that the message of comfort cannot be treated with joy and confidence because of the way in which the warning has been dealt with is a sure sign that the warning has been misunderstood. Conversely, to find that the warning has been deprived of its seriousness indicates that

[49]

the comfort has been misunderstood.Like the rest of the letter, this section has a positive purpose, and that is the hallmark of all apostolic ministry (see *2 Cor.* 10:8). It is an exhortation to possess 'the full assurance of hope' (6:11), and the writer is concentrating on the current condition of these professing believers, wanting it to be altered and improved. First, he diagnoses their condition and prescribes for it. Next, he issues a warning to underline the necessity of taking the medicine, and thirdly, he highlights a certainty to encourage them. In keeping with the perspective noted earlier (see pp. 34–9) of being on pilgrimage, we will think of *Pilgrims' Regress, Relapse* and *Progress* as we handle this passage.

9

Pilgrims' Regress

[11] Concerning him we have much to say, and it is hard to explain, since you have become dull of hearing. [12] For though by this time you ought to be teachers, you have need again for some one to teach you the elementary principles of the oracles of God, and you have come to need milk and not solid food. [13] For every one who partakes only of milk is not accustomed to the word of righteousness, for he is a babe. [14] But solid food is for the mature, who because of practice have their senses trained to discern good and evil.

[1] Therefore leaving the elementary teaching about the Christ, let us press on to maturity, not laying again a foundation of repentance from dead works and of faith toward God, [2] of instruction about washings, and laying on of hands, and the resurrection of the dead, and eternal judgment. [3] And this we shall do, if God permits (Heb. 5:11–6:3).

The term 'backsliding' is not used as frequently as it used to be. That might not be a bad thing because the word carries the suggestion that spiritual decline is something for which people are not responsible and that it is not serious. Both ideas are wrong. 'Backsliding' is more than 'not going on' and it may be more than 'slipping back'. The term may be *passé* but what it refers to is prevalent.

The teaching of the section before us is therefore much needed. It is made up of two interconnected parts. First, 5:11–14 describes the condition of the Hebrews. Secondly, 6:1–3 presents the remedy for it, as is indicated by the word 'Therefore' in 6:1. We will consider each of these sub-sections in order.

1. The Diagnosis

In 4:12–13 God's Word is described as being capable of uncovering the secrets of the human heart in an awe-inspiring way. This exposure of the condition of the Hebrews is an example of that. We will build up a general picture of their condition by commenting on some of the expressions in these verses.

i. *'Hard to explain' and 'dull of hearing'* (verse 11)

These words present the difficulty anticipated by the author and the reason for it. 'Hard to explain' is a translation of one word in the original text which is not found anywhere else in the Greek New Testament, although it was in common use at the time. It meant something that was inherently complex and even abstruse. But there is nothing in God's Word of that nature, though there is much that is profound. God is light and his Word is plain. The problem therefore does not arise either from the complexity of the subject or from any lack in the writer's understanding of it.

Where then does it lie? Entirely in the readers, and the expression 'dull of hearing' describes it. The word for 'dull' denotes sluggishness in movement; what should be working is hardly operating at all. Applied to the realm of Christian truth, it is a failure to appreciate and to respond appropriately. This is neither a physical disability nor an intellectual limitation. It is a moral-mental state, because to hear is not just to listen but also to understand and obey. It is like 'having ears but hearing not', and for that to be true of professing Christians is serious and dangerous (see 2:1; 3:7, 8,15; 4:1–2, 7).

ii. *'Have become' and 'by this time'* (verses 11–12)

The words 'have become' make clear that this condition of the Hebrews had a history. This means that there was a time when it began and, by implication, a time before that when it did not exist. Those addressed were therefore responsible for being what they now were. 'By this time' indicates that they had been Christians for some time and also that God had been gracious to them during that period. What therefore had happened ought never to have taken place. In fact, as the author goes on to state, the exact opposite should have occurred. He makes this clear by means of an analogy.

He refers to what characterizes a baby and someone who is an adult, assuming that, as there is development from the one to the other in natural life, so there is in the life divine. But the movement had gone in the reverse direction! Theirs was a second childhood, spiritually. What an irony!

iii. *'The first principles of the oracles of God'; 'the word of righteousness'* (verses 12–13)

The expression 'first principles' is literally 'the rudiments of the beginning', and the word for 'rudiments' can mean the alphabet. There is considerable discussion as to whether the writer is referring here and in 6:1–3 to the basic elements of an Old Testament faith or to the basics of Christianity. In our view the latter should be adopted because the writer speaks about 'the doctrine of Christ'. (The 'word of righteousness' is another way of referring to what the writer has in mind). Both point to the fact that 'the beginning' is made up of 'oracles' that is 'words' from God's own mouth.

We can only 'begin' in God's school by listening to the teacher and what he has spoken relates to 'righteousness'. This is a word that has been understood in a number of ways. In our view only two should be seriously considered and they do not have to be regarded as strict alternatives. The first is to let the immediate context, that is, verse 14, limit the meaning. This makes 'righteousness' to be ethical, relating only to right conduct. The other includes the dimension of acceptance with God as well, and in favour of that is the fact that 6:1–3 speaks again of elementary teaching about Christ, and 'faith' is mentioned along with repentance as initial matters.

There is nothing more basic than the ABC. It is what a child learns first. Without a grasp of letters, there is no way in which anyone can either read or write. Those addressed should have been able to take a Sunday school class. Instead, they were back in the crèche – almost. They were infants (verse 13).

Two features of infancy are highlighted and applied to those addressed. The first is related to diet and the second to discernment. An infant is neither able to chew nor choose. Mud goes into the mouth as well as milk. Similarly, immature Christians can show an aversion to spiritual food saying 'I don't like it', and an absence of moral principle saying 'What's wrong with . . . ?'

They should have become 'of full age' (verse 14). This is a translation of the word that is generally rendered by some form of the word 'perfect' or 'mature' as in 6:1. It represents a goal or end that has been reached, whatever that may be. Here it stands for what those addressed ought to be like. It is what would qualify them to be 'teachers' of others. Such people are able to take 'solid food', for example the teaching in chapter 7, and also to differentiate between good and bad, including not only right and wrong conduct but true and false doctrine as well.

The way to that goal is to have 'the senses exercised'. Pursuing the writer's analogy for a moment, let us think of a spiritual equivalent to the five senses which are so essential for human development. These are to be 'exercised', and that word gives us our term 'gymnasium'. A regular (daily) moral and spiritual workout is therefore required in order to gain an ability to understand things that come into the moral and spiritual realm and to use or repudiate them as appropriate. Such perception and ability is gained through being energetic and not lazy. It is the opposite of what led them to become 'dull of hearing'. The nuts and bolts of the understanding had become corroded; they had not been oiled regularly.

Such is the condition diagnosed. It is both surprising and serious. Instead of progressing and becoming able to teach the basics to others, they had regressed and needed to be re-taught the basics themselves. They should have become mature, able to apply knowledge gained to situations to be faced. Instead they were as impressionable and vulnerable as infants.

2. THE REMEDY (6:1–3)

This is expressed by means of a call to action which, interestingly, is in the passive voice. The Hebrews are therefore to act in co-operation with someone else, and, as the author includes himself in the duty to which he calls them, he is not that other. The verb which is used here is often used of the Holy Spirit, for example in Acts 2:2, Romans 8:14 and 2 Peter 1:21. It means to be carried along strongly, with the result that one can act vigorously and purposefully. This stands in sharp contrast to the aimless indolence of the Hebrews. 'The soul of the sluggard craves and gets nothing but the soul of the diligent shall be made fat' (*Prov.* 13: 4). There is a world of difference between wishing and working. The Spirit is therefore striving with the Hebrews – as he does with all believers. 'If God permits' means the same as our 'God willing'. It does not envisage the possibility that God might oppose those who comply with this call to press on to maturity. It does, however, recognize that no progress can be made without the gracious aid of his Spirit.

But how precisely is this command to be complied with? It is by leaving a laid foundation and leaning on favour given. Connecting the positive term 'leaving' with its negative counterpart, 'not laying again a foundation', in verse 2 amounts to an injunction to 'leave a laid foundation'. This does not of course mean leaving it behind in forgetfulness, but proceeding to build on it, having first laid it.

The foundation has already been described in 5:12 in relation to the truths of God's Word. Here it is described as 'the elementary teaching about the Christ'. Putting them together indicates that the truths of God's Word relate to the person of Jesus, as the Messiah. Faith therefore relates to truths about the Christ and not just to him as a person.

But it is also spoken of more specifically in terms of six component items. The last four (verse 2) are prefaced by the word 'instruction'. They are therefore doctrines. The first two, however, are not introduced in that way. They are therefore realities in the soul. The 'foundation' for a profession of faith is related not only to doctrine but also to experience. The best way (in our opinion) of understanding these six items is to note that they are set out in pairs and to think of them in relation to the apostles' preaching and teaching to Jews as it is described in the Acts of the Apostles.

Repentance and faith are the necessary and unvarying response to the preached message. Teaching about 'baptisms' refers to the distinctiveness of Christian baptism over against Jewish washings, and 'the laying on of hands' to the gift of the Holy Spirit and his ministry. Instruction about 'resurrection' and 'eternal judgment' relate to the certainty of an unending physical and glorious existence in the consummation of one's salvation, and the necessity of giving an account of one's life at the last day.

The call is therefore to stir oneself by the Spirit's aid and press on towards the heavenly goal. It is an anticipation of the well-known exhortation to run with endurance the race set before them and all God's people. A 'no man's land' is no place to be in a battle, and no one should comfort himself with the thought that he is in a backslidden condition.

10

Pilgrims' Relapse

⁴ For in the case of those who have once been enlightened and have tasted of the heavenly gift and have been made partakers of the Holy Spirit, ⁵ and have tasted the good word of God and the powers of the age to come, ⁶ and then have fallen away, it is impossible to renew them again to repentance, since they again crucify to themselves the Son of God, and put Him to open shame. ⁷ For ground that drinks the rain which often falls upon it and brings forth vegetation useful to those for whose sake it is also tilled, receives a blessing from God; ⁸ but if it yields thorns and thistles, it is worthless and close to being cursed, and it ends up being burned (Heb. 6:4–8).

Unanimity on the meaning of these verses has been lacking in the history of the church, and it still is. This fact should make us cautious as we form our own views about what they teach, and also willing to consider what others have to say about our conclusions. The method which we will follow is to concentrate on the major difficulty in these verses, namely 'falling away', considering what is being referred to. We will then ask two questions: 'From what can people fall away?', and 'Why can they not be renewed?' But we begin in a very general way by noting the literary form of the statement. To approach a difficult verse or passage from the broadest possible background is always a good method to follow.

1. THE FORM OF THE STATEMENT
There are four things to note about this:

   i. *It is made up of two related parts.*
Verses 7–8 illustrate part of verses 4–6. The type of ground that produces thorns and thistles corresponds to what is described in verses 4–6.

ii. *It records something actual (not theoretical).*

There is no conditional particle – 'if' – in the original text. Although it is true that the participle translated 'having fallen away' may have a conditional meaning because of its tense, the fact that it is one item in a list of participles (see verses 4–5) which cannot carry that meaning, argues against its being understood conditionally. Like 'having been enlightened', and so on, it should be translated 'having fallen away' and not 'if they fall away' as in KJV and NKJV. Something which has taken place is being referred to. To construe it, as some with Calvinistic convictions have, 'If they fall away, but, of course, being elect they will not, and cannot', is to add a distortion to a mistranslation. It deprives the warning of all its seriousness and makes its inclusion meaningless.

iii. *It is a negation (not an affirmation).*

Something is being denied here, not affirmed. It is the possibility of renewing any that fall away. While the statement does contain the possibility that some may fall away, there is no corresponding possibility that such may be restored. Just as what has been said about the 'if' has something to say to those who misuse Calvinist convictions, this says something to those with Arminian leanings, who affirm the possibility not only of 'falling from grace', but of being subsequently restored.

iv. *It uses impersonal language.*

The writer uses the third person in these verses, whereas it is the second person plural, 'you', that is prominent in 5:11–14, and the first person plural in 6:1–3. It is important to note this deliberate change and to appreciate its significance. While he is still addressing the same people as in 5:11–6:3, he is neither describing nor accusing them. These verses are therefore equivalent to a danger sign for example 'Precipice – Stay Well Clear!' They are a warning and not a charge.

2. THE FOCUS OF THE STATEMENT

Everything in these verses under consideration is related in some way or other to this matter of 'falling away'. What is it? As this is the hinge on which the whole statement turns, it is important to identify as accurately and precisely as possible what is in view. We therefore begin with the word itself and its use in this Epistle, before moving further into biblical material.

As is indicated by the English expression, we have here a verb 'fall' and also a preposition 'away'. In Greek they are joined together. The primary meaning of the verb is 'to fall', and it has already been used in 4:11 where it highlights Israel's disobedience in the wilderness as an historical event. It is also in view in 3:12 where, although we have a different verb, it has a complementary meaning. It indicates that there was something intentional about the incident – the 'falling away' was in reality a 'departing from'. This is confirmed in 6:4–6 by the preposition added to the verb, pointing to something or someone from which (or whom) the fall took place (see verse 4 below). The verb which is used in 3:12 gives us our term 'apostasy' or 'to apostatize'. That is the sin that is spoken of in these verses and also in 10: 26-31 and probably 12:16-17 as well.

What then is the nature of this sin of apostasy? There are two expressions in this letter which, taken together, enable a picture to be built up on this matter. They are 'departing from the living God' (3:12) and 'sinning wilfully' (10:26).

Taking the latter first, we need to call to mind that two types of sin are categorized in the Pentateuch in relation to the Mosaic covenant. First, there was *'sinning unintentionally'*. This was doing anything forbidden in the law, or failing to do anything required in it (*Lev.* 4:1, 13, 22 and *Num.* 15:22–29). Sacrifices were appointed for all those sins. Pardon and mercy were therefore available for those who had committed them. But there was also *'sinning presumptuously'*, literally 'sinning with a high hand' (see *Num.* 15:30–31). No sacrifice was appointed for such a sin; divine judgment descended on the perpetrator. This is the same as 'despising Moses' law'. It is not just an infringement of a command or any number of such, but a rejection of the living God and the covenant.

But such a sin is not only related to the Old Covenant arrangement. It has its counterpart under the New Covenant and, consequently, is more serious. Hebrews 10:29 describes this (see the discussion there). The distinctive features of the New

Covenant are listed there, and they become the object of someone's deliberate and manifested detestation, after he had professed to have experienced their benefit and worth! John Calvin describes apostasy as 'a total defection or falling away from the gospel when a sinner offends not God in some one thing, but entirely renounces his grace'. John Owen agrees and writes, 'It must consist in a total renunciation of all the constituent principles and doctrines of Christianity – in an avowed and professed manner.'

We take up now the two questions mentioned at the beginning. Facing them will bring this matter into a clearer light.

i. *From what can people apostasize?*

The essence of apostasy is a horrible unnaturalness. This is shown by the illustration in verses 7–8 where the ground that receives rain does not produce what is good and beneficial but what is bad and hurtful. Notice that the ground does not remain barren; it yields the opposite of what it should, given what it has received. An exact parallel is found in Isaiah 5: 1–7 where the vine (Israel) not only fails to produce grapes but yields wild grapes. Apostasy is something which stands in graphic and horrid contrast to the benefits and experiences listed in verses 4–6.

But how are these benefits to be understood? There is debate and uncertainty as to what is signified precisely by each. This is because the descriptive language is not specific, although it is impressive, and is intended to be so! However, there is, in the immediate context, something that quite clearly gives a perspective on what kind of benefits are in view in verses 4–6. It is the reference to 'better things' in verse 9. There are therefore better things than are listed in verses 4–5! An example of these is the Hebrews' service to Christians out of loving regard for God's name. Whatever verses 4–5 refer to, and these benefits are not to be minimized, they fall short of what belongs to saving grace. Here the rest of Scripture comes to our aid, because it indicates that there are extraordinary benefits and experiences which 'stony-ground hearers' received (*Mark* 4:16,18), which prophets and miracle workers possessed (*Matt.* 7:21-23) and there is also the alarming case of Judas himself. The mention of the Holy

Spirit in these verses should not lead us to think that regeneration or true conversion must be in view. Those who commit apostasy may therefore be said to fall from a height that is below the plateau of being regenerate. Truly, the least grace is a better insurance for heaven than the greatest gift.

ii. *Why can they not be renewed?*

There are two reasons given for this impossibility. They are two sides of the same coin. The one relates to the apostate and the other to God.

a. *Involved in the sin of apostasy is an action on oneself.*

Apostates re-crucify the Son of God 'to themselves' and 'before others', and although re-crucifying is a metaphor, the sin which it describes is real, and it has an effect. Having professed to embrace Christ crucified by faith, they now side with those who put him to death. They extinguish the light and love they professed to have and enter a lost darkness.

b. *Involved in the sin of apostasy is a reaction from God.*

Apostates are exposed to divine vengeance and judgment (10:31–32). God will therefore withhold repentance from them. Their sin makes them border on the curse because, having rejected Christ, declaring that he was worthy of death, they are 'rejected' and are 'to be burned' (6:8).

This warning therefore applies to all that have professed faith in Christ. No one is to conclude on any ground, but one, that he or she will not commit this sin. What is that ground? It is the daily pursuit of maturity. The use of the word 'for' at the beginning of verse 4 is a reminder that the immature Hebrews must take the medicine which has been prescribed for their immaturity, so that it does not get worse and turn into infidelity. The only way to avoid apostasy, ceasing to believe, is by continuing to believe in Jesus as the apostle and high priest, and to press on to know and serve him better. That is what the next section of this parenthesis majors on.

Pilgrims' Progress

⁹ But, beloved, we are convinced of better things concerning you, and things that accompany salvation, though we are speaking in this way. ¹⁰ For God is not unjust so as to forget your work and the love which you have shown toward His name, in having ministered and in still ministering to the saints. ¹¹ And we desire that each one of you show the same diligence so as to realize the full assurance of hope until the end, ¹² that you may not be sluggish, but imitators of those who through faith and patience inherit the promises. ¹³ For when God made the promise to Abraham, since He could swear by no one greater, He swore by Himself, ¹⁴ saying, 'I will surely bless you, and I will surely multiply you.' ¹⁵ And thus, having patiently waited, he obtained the promise. ¹⁶ For men swear by one greater than themselves, and with them an oath given as confirmation is an end of every dispute. ¹⁷ In the same way God, desiring even more to show to the heirs of the promise the unchangeableness of His purpose, interposed with an oath, ¹⁸ in order that by two unchangeable things, in which it is impossible for God to lie, we may have strong encouragement, we who have fled for refuge in laying hold of the hope set before us. ¹⁹ This hope we have as an anchor of the soul, a hope both sure and steadfast and one which enters within the veil, ²⁰ where Jesus has entered as a forerunner for us, having become a high priest forever according to the order of Melchizedek (Heb. 6: 9–20).

We have seen that it is helpful to bear in mind that this parenthetical section (5:11–6:20) is in the nature of a pastoral address. It comprises several elements. First, in 5:11–14, the writer describes the unspiritual condition of the Hebrews and identifies its cause. Secondly, and by way of remedy, he issues in 6:1–3 a fervent and pointed exhortation to diligent activity, in which he includes himself so as to reinforce its relevance. Next, in 6:4–8, he placards the terrible sin that can be committed within the visible church, as a warning to those addressed. Finally, having hedged them in by both exhortation and warning, he now identifies their current need and sets it in the context of God's grace in the Lord Jesus Christ, so opening up the way to the full assurance of faith.

The keynote of 6: 9–20 is encouragement; but this is not based on the writer's retracting, let alone contradicting, anything that he has just said. This is proved by his use of the present tense in verse 9, 'though we are speaking in this way'. The comfort is not, therefore, being given at the expense of the warning, which still stands and is not to be muted, let alone denied, in Christian teaching. It is rather based on the two-fold fact that 'better things' are true of those addressed, and that God has spoken a 'fuller word' to them than he had to their forefathers. That is the general framework for considering the encouraging address, but the writer begins by reminding them of their current weakness, which is to be remedied. Clutching the comfort is not to be a substitute for complying with that duty.

1. DIAGNOSIS

Whatever may be the precise nature of each of the good things listed in verses 4–5, which, as we have seen, are not to be minimized, the things that are now being specified are better. From a general point of view this is because they 'accompany salvation', while the others can be compatible with the curse (verse 8). What are these superior blessings? They are brotherly love, faith and hope (verses 10–12) – the triplets of saving grace.

It is clear that this love was genuine. It was no flush of emotionalism, but it had been in existence for some time, and it still was. What is more, it was directed to God's name and to the saints' need. God's name is the disclosure of his essential character. To love his name is therefore to love him because of who he is. To love the saints is to share in his love for them. This love is a self-giving, others-serving love, just like God's love.

However, although many 'cups of cold water' had been given - and at some risk to themselves (see 10:32–34), their faith and hope were moving sluggishly and this was not insignificant. They were still on the pathway of decline; it must not become a slippery slope. They might be a world away from those who would commit apostasy but they were certainly not like those who 'inherit' promised blessings, like Abraham and others to be mentioned in chapter 11. This deficiency was to be made good. Diligent obedience by way of *believing* God's Word and *expecting* its fulfilment, the twin areas of their weakness, was called for. Hope was to become full and faith was to become firm so that every promised blessing might become theirs. That is the safe path – away from apostasy and on to glory.

2. ENCOURAGEMENT

To encourage them onwards, the writer tells them something about himself and themselves, something about Abraham (and others not named) and two things about God. With regard to himself and themselves, he tells them that his desire is that they should make progress and informs them that all that is called for is that they direct the same energy into believing and hoping as into loving. They should cease to pick and choose among the commands of God.

With regard to Abraham, the writer illustrates what could and should be true of them. The fact that he quotes from Genesis 22:17 indicates that he is thinking of the particular occasion on Mount Moriah when Abraham's faith and hope in God were stretched by the command to sacrifice Isaac and also rewarded by a fuller self-disclosure of God to him. God will respond to those who trust him.

With regard to God, the encouragement to stake all on him repeatedly is based on two attributes of his character, that is about his name. Both are expressed negatively which is of course a way of emphasizing something positive. They are:

i. *God is unswervingly just* – verse 10.

God knows who are his servants even though they are weak and wayward. He does not forget service done to himself and to the saints. He appreciates both the deed done and the difficulty involved in doing it. 'Not forgetting' means that he holds it in his view – all of it, even the most insignificant deed, and that he will acknowledge it and reward it in a better world. And what is more, he will do so even though it is done by those whose faith and hope are declining!

ii. *God is unchangeably truthful* – verse 18.

'It is impossible for God [ever] to lie'. The same word is used here as in verse 4. It not only means that God does not lie but that, being God, he cannot do so, not even once. This is because to be divine is to be changeless and therefore truthful. Change creates a different condition or situation and that gives rise to a new set of possibilities. But God cannot change, and so things as he sees them, that is, as they really are, do not change either. Things do not appear differently to him in different circumstances as they do to human beings. He is; he knows; he speaks and neither denies nor distorts what is true by over-emphasis or under-emphasis. Everything he says can therefore be depended on utterly.

3. CERTAINTY

Two things about God are specified as being immutable. They are his promise and his oath. He is not only just and true but also good and kind, unspeakably so. It is not only the writer who desires the Hebrews to be full of hope and faith. God does too. In fact, the writer's desire is a reflection of God's. God wants to banish all uncertainty and doubt from his people so that they will have 'an anchor for the soul', and he has taken a most unusual step in order to do so. He has added an oath to his promise and so provided his people with two linchpins for their faith and hope.

There is an interesting Old Testament background to this procedure and it was probably in the mind of the writer. It can be found in Exodus 22:10–11. There, a neighbour is entrusted with the care of an animal by its owner. The animal is injured or stolen 'while no one is looking'. The neighbour is therefore unable to prove that he is not at fault, because there is no third party who can testify to what happened. In such an eventuality 'an oath before the LORD' to that effect by the neighbour was to be accepted by the owner, and no restitution was to be required. The 'oath given as confirmation is an end of every dispute' (verse 16). Clearly, the context envisaged is one in which lies and doubt are possible and may even ruin a relationship.

But God never lies, and yet his people often doubt his word of promise that expresses his purpose or eternal counsel. What unbelief! Is not God slighted? Yes, but he goes an extra mile in his self-revelation because he wants his people to have a 'strong encouragement'. Truly God is not a man! He is amazingly kind. But by whom can he swear, if an oath is always uttered in the name of someone greater? There is no one greater than himself. He knows when an oath is falsely taken and when one is not kept and he will require it. He is just and true, but will he swear by himself, as if he were not? Yes, he will, and he has, because he wants every one of his people to be as unwavering in their faith and hope as he is in his justice and truth.

But who are his people? They are described from two aspects in verses 17 and 18. From the side of God's electing purpose they are 'the heirs of the promise' and, by his effectual gospel call, he sets a hope before them; from their side, and because of their sin and liability to God's wrath, they 'have fled for refuge' to 'lay hold of' it. Jesus Christ is the real 'city of refuge' from the just avenger of sin (see *Num*. 35:6, 11–28)

A less than total hope and faith could be justified if God's Word were full of 'ifs' and 'buts'. But the covenant that God made with Abraham, he fulfilled in the Lord Jesus Christ. It says 'Surely blessing I will bless you and multiplying I will multiply you'. It is unconditional and unalterable. This irrevocable self-commitment by an immutable God concerning life in Jesus, the forerunner, who is 'within the veil', calls for a full assurance as the only appropriate response. Life in a fallen world is tempestuous and the soul needs an anchor that will not drag in the storm. Jesus has blazed a path to heaven and as king and priest will guard and guide all that trust in him. To anticipate a little, they are to 'fix (their) eyes on Jesus the author and perfecter of faith' (*Heb*. 12:2) and to 'run with endurance the race that is set before (them)', 'lay[ing] aside every encumbrance, and the sin which so easily entangles' them (12:1).

12

Melchizedek and Jesus

For this Melchizedek, king of Salem, priest of the Most High God, who met Abraham as he was returning from the slaughter of the kings and blessed him, ² to whom also Abraham apportioned a tenth part of all the spoils, was first of all, by the translation of his name, king of righteousness, and then also king of Salem, which is king of peace. ³ Without father, without mother, without genealogy, having neither beginning of days nor end of life, but made like the Son of God, he abides a priest perpetually. ⁴ Now observe how great this man was to whom Abraham, the patriarch, gave a tenth of the choicest spoils. ⁵ And those indeed of the sons of Levi who receive the priest's office have commandment in the Law to collect a tenth from the people, that is, from their brethren, although these are descended from Abraham. ⁶ But the one whose genealogy is not traced from them collected a tenth from Abraham, and blessed the one who had the promises. ⁷ But without any dispute the lesser is blessed by the greater. ⁸ And in this case mortal men receive tithes, but in that case one receives them, of whom it is witnessed that he lives on. ⁹ And, so to speak, through Abraham even Levi, who received tithes, paid tithes, ¹⁰ for he was still in the loins of his father when Melchizedek met him (Heb. 7: 1–10).

The Hebrews have been urged (see 3:1) to 'consider . . . Jesus [as their] high priest' and told (see 5:10, and again in 6:20) that in order to do this properly they should think about Melchizedek as well as Aaron, in fact more about the former than the latter. In these verses the writer proceeds to explain how that can and should be done. We will take the words at the beginning of verse 4, 'Consider how great this man was', as our way into this section.

1. MELCHIZEDEK'S GREATNESS SUMMARIZED (verses 1–3)
We begin by noting the structure of these opening verses. They contain a number of relative clauses, all of which related to the statement, 'For this Melchizedek . . . remains a priest continually'. The central theme is therefore Melchizedek's unending priesthood and everything else that is said bears upon this subject. The last of these clauses says, 'made like the Son of God', and that indicates that all that has gone before has some relevance to Jesus.

What is the basis for this correspondence? It is expressed in the participle 'made'. The verb is in the passive voice which means that something has been done to Melchizedek, so that he might resemble the Son of God. The resemblance is therefore not of Melchizedek's own making.

A question therefore arises as to who 'made' this resemblance. Is it the writer of the letter, we may wonder? Although he is obviously involved because he expressed the similarity, it is obvious that he was not the one responsible for it in the first place, because he quotes the words of someone else to that effect. That other is God himself whose word the writer has quoted in 5:6 and quotes again in verse 17 of this chapter. God made Melchizedek resemble Jesus. But how did he do that? He did it by what he said, and did not say, about Melchizedek in the Old Testament in Genesis 14:18–22, and especially Psalm 110:4. Melchizedek is therefore 'made like the Son of God' in the Old Testament text, by God's own word about him. He is therefore a *type*.

Some important conclusions can be drawn from this for the whole study of types in the Bible. Positively, God makes types by his Word, and they are founded on a real correspondence between one person or thing and another in the Bible, most often between things in the Old and New Testaments. Types are not the result of a reader's fanciful imagination. They rest on a solid textual and theological similarity.

The word 'type' is associated with a verb that means 'to strike a blow so as to leave a mark'. It is used in a physical or material sense in John 20:25 of the 'print' of the nails, and in Acts 7:43–44 of things produced from moulds; and psychologically, of the wounding of the conscience in 1 Corinthians 8:12. Adam was a type of him who was to come (*Rom.* 5:14) and the things which happened to the Israelites in the wilderness are types, or examples, for our learning (*1 Cor.* 10:6, 11).

It is interesting to note that while the writer of this letter does use the word 'type' in a technical way, as in the above texts (see 8:5), in 9:24 he uses the word 'antitype' for the same thing as well. This is not a confusion of concepts but only a stylistic variation. His consistent way of thinking is in terms of God having produced 'heavenly things' by his saving purpose (see 9:23, and comment there), and of patterns or moulds of them being made in the Old Testament before the finished article appears in the New Testament.

The word 'copy' has the advantage of bringing to mind an original, and an 'example' points away from itself. So just as John chose the word 'sign' in his gospel because the Jews were fascinated with seeing miracles, so the writer to the Hebrews wants to focus the attention of his readers on the heavenly and not the earthly. In like manner, present day evangelicals can be taken up with finding earthly types, or types of events on earth that will have a fulfilment in the end-times. True understanding of God's Word and right conduct suffer in such a pursuit of the fanciful at the expense of the practical, and the visible at the expense of the heavenly.

So Melchizedek is a type of Jesus. In what respects? In terms of what is said, and not said, about him in the Old Testament which the writer of *Hebrews* draws attention to. We can summarize it by saying that they relate to clear statements in the Old Testament and also to equally clear silences there, all confirmed by subsequent revelation, in this case Psalm 110:4 – the verse from the Old Testament which the writer used most often and which coloured the whole of his thinking about Jesus.

i. *Clear Statements*

The data in these first two verses are all taken from Genesis 14. Melchizedek was an ordinary human being. He is called 'a man' in verse 3. To identify him with a pre-incarnate appearance of Christ destroys the necessary correspondence between type and antitype and, in addition, there is no hint of a theophany in Genesis 14. As his name is Semitic in character, we can deduce that he belonged to the line of Shem, through which the blessing of God would flow (*Gen.* 9: 26).

Melchizedek lived in the patriarchal era. He met Abraham on a particular occasion. 'El Elyon' was the name of the God he served and Abraham knew. His name and that of the seat of his rule have a meaning, which is that peace for a king's subjects is connected in some way with his own righteousness. Special emphasis is placed on the fact that he was both king and priest – a unique combination of official ministries that was subsequently forbidden in the Old Testament.

All this indicates that the writer does not set aside the plain historical data of the text in pursuit of some 'higher' meaning in it. That is the single big difference between typological interpretation and allegory. Not only does the latter sit loose to the original context of a verse, but it glories in setting it aside as it spins some interpretation which has no connection with it. A well-known (notorious) example of this is the identification of the two coins given by the Samaritan to the innkeeper in Luke 10:35 with the two sacraments.

ii. *Striking Omissions*

This may seem to be a dangerous concession to make. But we are not talking about something that God did not see fit to provide in the scriptural record, which we would like to know about, and (perish the thought) think we can supply. Instead, it is something whose absence is pointed out in Scripture itself. Imagine that Genesis 1–14 was all that we had of the Bible. What would we not know about Melchizedek that we would know about others? We would not know that he was born or that he died, or who his parents were, and these were details that Moses was recording about others. So why is it that in a book like Genesis (literally 'Beginning'), which contains ten genealogies, no such details about Melchizedek are given?

The answer is that this information was not recorded because God was making a mould. He was introducing someone who, being 'without father, without mother, without genealogy . . . beginning of days or end of life' would stand in stark contrast to the later insistence on genealogical qualifications for the priests, and who would anticipate the unending priesthood of his eternal Son to all who read the Old Testament with understanding. That is why Melchizedek bursts on the scene like a meteor and, as suddenly, disappears again. Even he was *temporary*!

2. MELCHIZEDEK'S GREATNESS EXPANDED (verses 4–10)

Some standard of comparison is always necessary for the measurement of greatness and the writer sees that the history recorded in Genesis 14 supplies him with a perfect yardstick for this purpose. Abraham! There was no one greater in the history of Israel or in the thinking of the Jewish people. John the Baptist knew that (*Matt.* 3: 9), so did Jesus (*John* 8:33, 39), and so would the Hebrews. A true idea of Melchizedek's greatness can therefore be obtained by reference to Abraham.

The order in which the writer arranged his words in verse 3 expresses the amazement that he wanted the Hebrews to feel as he presented and drew out the details of the comparison. This is reproduced by the NIV's helpful insertion of the word 'even' before 'Abraham' in verse 4. We will consider Melchizedek's greatness under the headings of his majesty and his ministry, remembering all the while that he is representing the 'greater greatness' of the Son.

i. *His majesty*

In these verses the writer aims to point up Melchizedek's majesty. But he does so by way of implication from a number of epithets and clauses that describe the greatness of Abraham. Only once does he describe Melchizedek explicitly, in verse 8, saying, in the present tense, 'he lives on'. This is in contrast with the mortal Levites, and foreshadows Jesus.

What are the aspects of Abraham's greatness? First, he is called 'the patriarch' (verse 4), as if there were no others. But there were. There was Isaac, Jacob and even David (*Acts* 2:29) and others too (*Acts* 7: 8). But he was alone when God called him (*Isa.* 51:2). Secondly, he is described as having 'the promises' (verse 6). He was the one to whom God first gave the promises of land, nation and seed (*Gen.* 12: 1–6) and it was he who was to be the means of divine blessing or judgment to others. Genesis 14 contains an example of both these aspects in relation to the conquest of the kings and the deliverance of Lot. Thirdly, he was the progenitor of all Israel. The Levites and the members of all the other tribes were present, seminally, in him (verse 10). But Melchizedek assumed a higher rank than Abraham and Abraham did not demur.

ii. *His ministry*

This is expressly stated in terms of what Melchizedek did to Abraham. He pronounced a blessing on him and took tithes from him. Both were priestly functions and took place in the context of worship.

To bless is not to wish someone well, but to possess and confer a benefit, and it is inevitably the case that the one who is blessed is less than the one who blesses. Acting in the name of God Most High, Melchizedek conveyed something to rich and powerful Abraham. He reminded him of who it was that had given him the victory, and in so doing he conveyed to Abraham a further assurance of God's favour. That is priestly activity.

In turn, Abraham receives from the king of Salem all that he has to give him, but refuses to receive anything from the king of Sodom. In addition, he gives tithes in thanks to God's high priest and does so of all the riches that God has given him, and Melchizedek receives those thank offerings in God's name. Melchizedek was therefore acting as a mediator of God's blessing to Abraham and of his gratitude to God. So does Jesus who acts in a greater way in the name of the Most High God.

The conclusion to this argument should not need to be stated. It is inescapable. If Abraham the forefather of Israel and all the priests, humbled himself before Melchizedek, then so should the Hebrews before the one whom Melchizedek typified, Jesus the Son of God. So should we – and the church of today – everywhere!

13

Jesus and Aaron

[11] Now if perfection was through the Levitical priesthood (for on the basis of it the people received the law), what further need was there for another priest to arise according to the order of Melchizedek, and not be designated according to the order of Aaron? [12] For when the priesthood is changed, of necessity there takes place a change of law also. [13] For the one concerning whom these things are spoken belongs to another tribe, from which no one has officiated at the altar. [14] For it is evident that our Lord was descended from Judah, a tribe with reference to which Moses spoke nothing concerning priests. [15] And this is clearer still, if another priest arises according to the likeness of Melchizedek, [16] who has become such not on the basis of a law of physical requirement, but according to the power of an indestructible life. [17] For it is witnessed of Him, 'Thou art a priest forever according to the order of Melchizedek.' [18] For, on the one hand, there is a setting aside of a former commandment because of its weakness and uselessness [19] (for the Law made nothing perfect), and on the other hand there is a bringing in of a better hope, through which we draw near to God. [20] And inasmuch as it was not without an oath [21] (for they indeed became priests without an oath, but He with an oath through the One who said to Him, 'The Lord has sworn and will not change His mind, "Thou art a priest forever"'); [22] so much the more also Jesus has become the guarantee of a better covenant. [23] And the former priests, on the one hand, existed in greater numbers, because they were prevented by death from continuing, [24] but

He, on the other hand, because He abides forever, holds His priesthood permanently. [25] Hence also He is able to save forever those who draw near to God through Him, since He always lives to make intercession for them. [26] For it was fitting that we should have such a high priest, holy, innocent, undefiled, separated from sinners and exalted above the heavens; [27] who does not need daily, like those high priests, to offer up sacrifices, first for His own sins, and then for the sins of the people, because this He did once for all when He offered up Himself. [28] For the Law appoints men as high priests who are weak, but the word of the oath, which came after the Law, appoints a Son, made perfect forever (Heb. 7:11–28).

G od is not erratic and he never acts impulsively. But he often surprises and perplexes his people. Sometimes, this is because of the suddenness and abundance of his answers to their prayers, and they become like 'those who dream' (*Psa.* 126:1) or those who 'could not believe for joy and marvelled' (*Luke* 24:41).

On other occasions, however, it is because they have failed to notice indications that he has given them of what he is going to do. As a result they think that God is acting in contradiction of what he has previously said and done. That is what the Jews thought Jesus was doing, namely, destroying the 'law and the prophets' (*Matt.* 5:17; see also *Acts* 6:13–14). Even those who believed in Jesus as Messiah were not entirely free from this outlook, as can be seen from Peter's difficulty with the vision which was given to prepare him for the reception of the Gentiles into the kingdom of God (*Acts* 10:9–17). Similarly, in this chapter, the writer points out to the Hebrews that the descendants of Aaron had been replaced by a priest who resembled Melchizedek, and they ought not to have been surprised at that, much less perplexed. It had been planned and announced.

We will consider this section under two headings namely *the imperfect priesthood* and *the perfect priest*. Following a sustained comparison between the priesthood which descended from Aaron and that of Jesus (verses 11–24), the writer speaks rapturously about the unsurpassable majesty and ministry of Jesus as high priest (verses 25–28).

1. THE IMPERFECT PRIESTHOOD

What the writer says about the imperfection of this priesthood is not at the expense of the dignity of its institution. Four features of its greatness are readily acknowledged.

i. *It was related to law* (verse 11).

The people received the gift of the priesthood as part of the law, that is, the covenant made with them at Mount Sinai. It was therefore no human invention, but divinely authorized. So closely was it connected with the law that there could not be any change in it without the law being affected, as is indicated in verse 12.

ii. *It was revealed through Moses* (verse 14).

He was the one who made these things known, as from God (*Exod.* 28:1). He was the founder of the theocratic community.

iii. *It was restricted to the line of Aaron* (verses 11 and 16).

A special class of men were designated to this office and ministry and to all the privileges and duties that went with it (*Num* 18:1). Lineal descent was the all-important qualification.

iv. *It regulated worship at the altar* (verse 13).

The priests received the sacrifices brought by the worshippers (*Lev.* 1-7) and the high priest ministered on the Day of Atonement (*Lev.* 16)

The writer thus acknowledges all that was true about the Levitical priesthood within the context of the covenant made at Sinai, and in no respect does he diminish its centrality or importance. But he roundly asserts that it was imperfect and goes on to speak of its abrogation as a consequence.

The way by which the author points this out and proves it, is important to note. The Old Testament is once more his authority. He uses an Old Testament prediction and its fulfilment in New Testament history.

He describes the imperfection that characterized the authorized priesthood (verse 19) as 'weakness and uselessness'. This points to a flaw in its nature that results in a lack of effectiveness. It is a big claim. How does he justify this, especially as he has just spoken in terms of its divine origin? He does so on the basis of his favourite Old Testament text, namely Psalm 110: 4, which he quotes in verse 17 and introduces solemnly as the testimony of God. The announcement that a priest would come, patterned after Melchizedek and not Aaron, was a big, broad hint about the inadequacy of the Levitical priesthood, and it effected a change of law.

So he does not declare the imperfection of the Levitical priesthood on the basis of his own thinking but on the authority of God who had instituted it. He it was who announced that it was to be superseded. He did that in the time of David while it was in its heyday – and most of his people had not noticed it.

But what was the perfection that the law and the priesthood could not provide, even though it was divinely authorized? It is described in terms of 'a better hope', which is that of 'drawing near to God'. Approach to the tabernacle and, by implication, the temple, amid all their distinctive splendour, could not bring people near to God. This is further explained in 9:19 and 10:1. What went on there lacked substance and merit. It was incapable of saving. This was because God never intended it to save, but to point away from itself to Jesus who alone could and would deal with sin. A worshipper could therefore come to a duly ordained priest with a sacrifice which matched up to ritual regulation in every detail, but that by itself did not secure acceptance with God and his pardon and cleansing. This is because such a sacrifice could not take away sin (10:4).

As a result the priestly law was abrogated. By placing a word which means 'cancelled' at the beginning of verse 18, the writer emphasizes its meaning and draws the attention of his readers to it. The same word is used by him in 9:26 to describe the dismantling and demolishing effect that Christ's death has on sin.

The New Testament either elevates the Old Testament order of things or abrogates it. It does not just restate it. Indeed, that is impossible, because of the greater light which the New casts on the Old. Abrogation is what has happened to the levitical priesthood, and that was effected just as it was inaugurated – by the word of the One who had appointed it. No other annulment would be valid. Again, Psalm 110:4 provides the evidence for this, and what was thus predicted was fulfilled. The priest from 'another tribe' did 'arise' (verses 14–16).

2. THE PERFECT PRIEST

There is a double shift in these verses that is important to note. First, there is the change from the 'order' of Aaron to that of Melchizedek and with it from the tribe of Levi to that of Judah; and secondly, there is the change from 'the many' priests to 'the one' (verses 23–24). These changes are summed up in the word 'another' which means, not just someone else, but 'another of a different kind'. It is because of what this difference connotes that this one priest can do what the many could not. What distinguishes this one priest from all others is 'the power of an endless [indestructible] life' (verse 16). That is the answer to the 'weakness and [therefore] uselessness' of the old priesthood and the law which gave authority to its ministrations. This one priest could deal with sin and therefore with death its result, because, as the Son, he could not die. This is indeed a 'better hope', reflected in the oath that installed him in office and the life that characterizes his ministry. This is in stark contrast to the institution and imperfection of the old arrangement.

i. *Installation*

Verses 20 and 21 point out that God did not appoint the levitical priests to office with an oath as he did in the case of Jesus. We have seen from the use of Psalm 95 and Genesis 22 in chapters 3 and 6 of this epistle respectively that an oath is an asseveration of changeless intent and will not be revoked. So anxious is the writer to make this inescapably clear that he takes the words 'and will not change his mind' from Numbers 23:19 and inserts them in his quote of Psalm 110:4. Jesus will therefore never have a successor. He ever lives and God's oath stands.

The permanence of this appointment, however, is not merely to be connected with the 'the better hope' of access to God which Jesus provides but with his being 'the guarantee of a better covenant' (verse 22). This is the first time that the word 'covenant' is used in *Hebrews*, and it is therefore not without significance that the writer does not use the word 'Mediator' to describe Jesus' connection with it. This is doubtless because the Old Covenant had 'a mediator' (see *Gal.* 3:19), but he was not one who could secure any of its benefits. Jesus is a 'guarantee' or a 'surety', that is, one who legally substitutes for others, undertaking to perform all obligations required and discharge whatever liabilities are due for every infringement of its terms. Jesus is that kind of 'mediator' for the 'better' or 'new' covenant. He pays debts and secures blessings in full, in both cases!

ii. *Intercession*

The verses that conclude this chapter are a jubilant testimony to the uniqueness of Jesus as high priest. Not being weak himself through sin (see verse 28), but personally holy, neither corrupting anyone nor being defiled by anyone, he could offer one sacrifice for sins. Having done that, he is highly exalted to where he may intercede for sinners. He is exactly the kind of high priest that weak sinners need. Verse 25 is the statement which sums up better than any other so much of what the writer has been saying. We will use it for that purpose and think of the endless life of Jesus Christ, his ceaseless intercession and the boundless salvation which results for all who come to God through him – and keep doing so.

iii. *Endless life* – 'He always lives'

This is not a reference to the fact of his physical resurrection from the dead with a deathless life but to the fact that being a divine person, the Son, he is immortal in the first place. His life is indestructible (verse 16). But did he not die, really? Yes, he did. How then does his death affect his priesthood? When Aaron was about to die, did not Moses divest him of his priestly garments and put them on Eleazar his son who succeeded him (*Num.* 20:25–29, especially verse 28)? How then does Jesus' death not terminate his priesthood? Because it only affected his human nature and it was the way by which he actually entered into his priestly office, dealing with sin by offering himself as a sacrifice to God.

iv. *Ceaseless intercession* – 'He always lives to make intercession'

This is what he does with his endless life. He continually seeks from his Father those blessings that he procured by his death for his people. His prayer in John 17 is an example of this intercession. He provides them with his life-giving Spirit, instructs, protects and enriches them and brings them to glory. He prays for them when they are not praying for themselves, both in advance of their needing help and when they have failed, as in the well-known case of Simon Peter (*Luke* 22:31–32).

v. *Boundless salvation* – 'He is able to save forever'

The choice of the term 'forever' is an attempt to translate a Greek idiom. It is not inaccurate, because included in the original is the word for 'end'. But a question may be raised as to whether it is adequate, because the word for 'end' can also mean 'goal'. Somewhat parallel expressions are found in John 13:1, with reference to Christ's love, and 1 Thessalonians 2:16, with reference to God's wrath. Something can therefore be said in favour of the quaint rendering of the KJV – 'to the uttermost', which includes both aspects.

What is in view here is the impermissibility of setting any limit to the salvation that Christ completely procured in his death and lives to bestow in its totality. His people dare not even draw a line in their own minds, saying to themselves, 'He helped me today, but will he tomorrow?', or, 'He helped in this need, but will he in that?', or, 'He forgave me this sin before, but will he do so again?' He will ever live as their Saviour. He will never fail them or forget them.

14

A Better Ministry

*Now the main point in what has been said is this: we have such
a high priest, who has taken His seat at the right hand of
the throne of the Majesty in the heavens, ² a minister in the
sanctuary, and in the true tabernacle, which the Lord pitched,
not man. ³ For every high priest is appointed to offer both gifts
and sacrifices; hence it is necessary that this high priest also
have something to offer. ⁴ Now if He were on earth, He would
not be a priest at all, since there are those who offer the gifts
according to the Law; ⁵ who serve a copy and shadow of the
heavenly things, just as Moses was warned by God when he
was about to erect the tabernacle; for, 'See,' He says, 'that you
make all things according to the pattern which was shown you
on the mountain.' ⁶ But now He has obtained a more excellent
ministry, by as much as He is also the mediator of a better
covenant, which has been enacted on better promises* (Heb.
8:1–6).

Once more the preacher pauses as he writes his sermon. Why
does he do so this time? It is for the same sort of reason as was
noted in connection with 5:11-6:20. He has in mind those to whom
he is writing. But this time he does not introduce a parenthesis; he
wants to crystallize his message for them.

In sermons a preacher will often say to his hearers 'This is the
main thing I want you to note', or some such phrase. He does so
to alert them to the importance of what they are about to hear in
the hope and prayer that they will be particularly attentive, grasp
what they hear and meditate on it. That is what the opening
words of this chapter amount to, and it shows that the writer is

[80]

not content just to state truth correctly. He wants to inform minds, so as to affect lives. This is why he pauses momentarily and speaks as succinctly as he can, distilling the essence of his message.

The opening word of the first verse in this chapter which is translated 'main point' is derived from the noun for 'head'. It occurs in the Greek translation of the well-known expression, 'the beginning of wisdom', in the Book of Proverbs. It is used in a figurative sense for 'beginning and end', that is, the essential feature. An equivalent in the western world would be 'the heart of the matter', rather than 'the head'. But God's truth is for head and heart, whatever it has to say – and especially when it speaks about the Lord Jesus Christ who is the theme of these verses.

As the writer is here summarizing what he wants to say to the Hebrews, the question arises as to what this 'main point' is, and how much of his letter it includes. Is it only what is stated in these two verses, or perhaps the whole of chapter 7, or even more? Because the theme of 8:1–2 is the 'high priest', many have assumed it must be the case that the teaching of 4:14–7:28 is to be included in its scope, because the same subject is dealt with there. But is there even more? Going backwards through the letter, do not 3:1, and 2:17–18, and 1:3, also bear on this very subject? And going towards the end, do not 8:3–6, 9:1–28; 10:1–20; 12:24, and 13:12 do so as well? In the light of all these references it becomes possible to see that the 'main point' of 8:1–2 is the central theme of the entire written sermon. What precedes it leads up to it, and what follows flows from it.

But what is it? What is this 'main point'? It is not just that Christians have a high priest, but that he is *in heaven*. This unique and all-embracing truth is foundational to everything else. It is what differentiates the Christian high priest from all other priests and it is what the writer wants to say and wants his readers to realize and appreciate.

We will divide our consideration of this section into two parts. First, we will look at the specific affirmation in verses 1 and 2, and secondly, at the supporting argument in verses 3–6. Both of these explain the 'more excellent ministry' referred to in verse 6.

1. THE BETTER MINISTRY AFFIRMED (verses 1–2)
This is done from the following three angles.

i. *The place where he ministers*
This is specified as being in 'the heavens'. What does this plural noun mean? It is used in 1:10 and 4:14 where it represents all the supra-terrestrial realms. In this sense it is synonymous with the word 'worlds' in 1:2 and 11:3 and refers to the sum total of created reality. But is that what it means in this verse? Surely not! In 8:1 'the heavens' is where 'the throne of the Majesty' is found, and also the sanctuary which 'the Lord erected'. This realm is therefore higher or further than all that is created through which the Lord passed (see 7:26). It is 'heaven itself' that is in view here. It is the very 'presence of God' (9:24).

ii. *The posture which he adopts*
Our high priest is 'seated' in the presence of God and 'at the right hand' of his majesty. This word 'seated' contrasts markedly with what the Aaronic high priests were permitted to do They functioned representatively for the people in the Holy of Holies, the earthly and symbolic throne-room of God, but were required to stand there because their work was never complete. It needed to be repeated annually because it never really dealt with sin. But the perfect sacrifice of our High Priest is at one and the same time the means by which he puts an end to sin, and enters into his unending priesthood. He therefore sits, with no more work to do by way of obedience to God to qualify him either to deal with sin or to intercede for and guard his people. He did all that was required for all that and therefore sat down at the invitation of God, and 'at his right hand', the place of power. His sacrifice is accepted and he is enthroned. Therefore his intercession and guardianship must prevail.

iii. *The purpose he executes*
But 'heaven' does not only *stand in distinction from* all that is spatial and temporal. It also *corresponds to* what is merely symbolic or pictorial. There is a real ('true' in verse 2 means 'real') tabernacle and a throne. The 'true' tabernacle is the actual dwelling place of God, and there he personally meets with his worshipping

[82]

people. The same can be said about the 'throne'. It is the seat from which God actually rules.

Heaven is not in Jerusalem, or Zion, or anywhere else for that matter. It is 'the place' where divine decrees are put into effect and where worship is offered to God in face-to-face fellowship with him. It is 'the place' where those things which have eternal value and consequences exist and are really done. And the high-priest is officiating there, putting God's decrees into effect and praying for the people of God. He is the king-priest; ruling over the earth and interceding in heaven with equal effectiveness.

This is why the writer not only wrote, 'We have a high priest', but, 'We have *such* a high priest', putting the adjective 'such' after the verb 'have' for the sake of conveying a grateful confidence to his readers. As heaven is where the great high priest is, and ruling and interceding are what he is doing there, his non-visibility, in comparison with the high profile of the Jewish priests, should not cause the Hebrews any difficulty at all. But it did, and so the writer presses on in his desire to capture their minds and hearts with this truth.

2. THE BETTER MINISTRY ARGUED FOR

He continues with this theme by entering into an argument with the Hebrews on the basis of their own thinking. The line of reasoning which he uses consists of a supposition which his readers favour, namely, 'Now if he were on earth' (verse 4), and a conclusion drawn from it, in which he proceeds to show what its consequences would be, if it were true. By this stylistic device, he not only shows how far from the truth the thinking of the Hebrews is, but how inferior to the truth it is. It is far, far better that the high-priest is not on earth. It means that he has 'a more excellent ministry' than those who are. We will consider the supposition and its correction in turn.

i. *The supposition – 'If he were on earth'*

Verse 3 declares that bringing offerings to God is a 'must' of high-priestly activity (see 5:1–3) and that this requirement also applies to 'this high priest'. The fact that he is not named is not a mark of disrespect. It stresses the universality of the requirement and enables the writer to point out that if 'he' (Jesus) were on earth he would not be allowed to minister along with those who were then serving in the temple. Why not? The answer has already been given to this question in 7:13–14 where it is pointed out that Jesus was not a member of the tribe of Levi but was a descendant of Judah, and so he would have been excluded from priestly service by the law.

But the writer is not content with making a telling point by way of inference. He points out that those who were at the time ministering in the temple were doing so in relation to what was only 'a copy and shadow of heavenly things'. They were only able to deal with representations of heavenly things which, though appointed and designed by God, were only symbolic, not substantial. Who would want a high priest to minister in connection with shadows? Verses 1 and 2 have shown that Jesus ministers in relation to heavenly things themselves.

ii. *The correction – 'having obtained a more excellent ministry'.*

This more excellent ministry will be described later in relation to a better covenant, better promises, a greater tabernacle and a better sacrifice, and these will be considered in turn. Here we must not overlook the verb 'obtained'. It gathers to itself the two aspects of our Lord's suitability to be 'such a high-priest' which were mentioned in the previous chapter. The first is that, as required by law, he was appointed to this ministry by God, but with the extra feature of an irrevocable oath (see 7:21). Secondly, by doing all that God required of him he 'became perfect', that is, he acquired, personally and exclusively, a fitness, a capacity to be and do all his people would ever need. He is permanently installed and personally sufficient. Help from others is not only superfluous but blasphemous. Though he is out of his people's sight, they are never out of his. He is never beyond the reach of their supplications or they beyond his prevailing and beneficial intercession.

Hopefully, this conclusive and glorious argument convinced the Hebrews. But we should not judge them too harshly. We need to take this to heart too. Fascination with ritual and priestly activity has, throughout the centuries, diverted the attention of Christians from the ministry of Jesus in heaven and led them to feel deprived if they do not have something similar. It has even prompted them to devise it.

Today, the church finds herself surrounded and even invaded by religious syncretism and priestcraft. But how can the alleged benefits of any religion compare with true Christianity? How can the most richly-robed human (let alone a gaudily-bedecked image) be even ranked alongside our great high priest ministering 'at the right hand of the throne of the majesty in the heavens'? What is the highest altar in any ornate and impressive cathedral compared with 'the tabernacle which the Lord pitched'? What is a crucifix or *pietà* compared with a Saviour who is enthroned because his sacrifice for sin has been accepted by God, the Judge of all?

There is not only no comparison at all between these, but there is a great blasphemy in all such artefacts.

15

A Better Covenant

⁷ For if that first covenant had been faultless, there would have been no occasion sought for a second. ⁸ For finding fault with them, He says, 'Behold days are coming, says the Lord, when I will effect a new covenant with the house of Israel and with the house of Judah; ⁹ not like the covenant which I made with their fathers on the day when I took them by the hand to lead them out of the land of Egypt; for they did not continue in My covenant, and I did not care for them, says the Lord. ¹⁰ For this is the covenant that I will make with the house of Israel after those days, says the Lord: I will put My laws into their minds, and I will write them upon their hearts. And I will be their God, and they shall be My people. ¹¹ And they shall not teach every one his fellow-citizen, and every one his brother, saying, "Know the Lord," for all shall know Me, from the least to the greatest of them. ¹² For I will be merciful to their iniquities, and I will remember their sins no more.' ¹³ When He said, 'A new covenant,' He has made the first obsolete. But whatever is becoming obsolete and growing old is ready to disappear (Heb. 8:7–13).

We are going to examine this basic and far-reaching statement in three steps or stages. First, we will identify which covenants are being referred to. Secondly, we will compare (and contrast) their respective promises. Finally, we must highlight what it is that makes the one so much better than the other.

1. IDENTIFICATION
i. *Which two covenants?*
There is no difficulty at all about identifying one of the

covenants spoken of. It is the one whose Mediator is Jesus, as verse 6 indicates. But what is the other? It is not enough to think of the Old Testament in general, as there is more than one covenant recorded there. Which one is in view? It is crucial not to make a mistake on this point, as the covenant that is contrasted with the one Jesus guarantees is now abrogated. Verse 9 answers this question by declaring that this other covenant was made in connection with the Exodus from Egypt. It is therefore the Sinaitic covenant. It is not the one made with Abraham which, according to Galatians 3, is fulfilled in the 'better' one, and is therefore in greater force, not less.

But how could the writer talk of just two covenants, as if there were no others? The answer is that there were only two arrangements which God introduced in order to structure the corporate life of his people, including the whole of their relationship to him, and his to them. The first of these refers to the nation, Israel, and the second to the Christian church.

ii. *How are they described?*

They are correlated by means of two sets of adjectives. These are *first and second*, and *old and new*. We consider each set.

a. *First and second* (verse 7)

These terms relate, of course, to time and order. The one was introduced before the other. It was because of this that the earlier could typify the later.

b. *Old and new* (verse 13)

These terms relate to quality and validity, or authority. The introduction of 'the new' makes the first covenant 'old'. The NIV rendering brings this out helpfully in its translation of verse 13. It reads: 'By calling this covenant "new" he has made the first obsolete.' So the Christian church is not to regulate itself by the covenant made at Sinai as a 'package'.

2. CONTRAST

Now that we know what is being referred to we can proceed to the contrast, which we will delineate in two stages. First, we will concentrate on what is said regarding the Old Covenant, and then, against that background, look at what is said about the better one.

i. *The character of the Old Covenant.*

As it is of the essence of making a fair comparison or contrast to do justice to all sides, we begin by what is said in favour of the Old Covenant. Two things are said about it in verse 9.

a. *It was a covenant that God made.*

The verb 'enacted' in verse 6 refers to the unilateral act of a lawful sovereign. No haggling took place and no bargain was struck. Its terms were authoritative in the highest sense.

b. *It was made in grace with a chosen and delivered people.*

Verse 7 says that God 'took them by the hand' to lead them out. This is marvellous condescension. Though the covenant presented requirements that related to their life towards God and each other, including the stranger, it was not destitute of grace. It arose out of grace and it had its promises.

But granted all this, what must be said on the other side? This Old Covenant was 'faulty' (verse 7) and 'fading' (verse 13). These are bold statements. Can something which is introduced by God be faulty and fading, without an adverse reflection being cast on him? Only if he declares it so. We have seen this kind of argument already in chapter 7 in connection with the priesthood where Psalm 110:4 is pointed to as God's own announcement that a better priesthood was going to come. So here, Jeremiah 31:31–34 is quoted to show that a better covenant was on the way.

Let us focus on these two 'defects' of the first, the Old Covenant, and think of its *impotence* and its *impermanence*.

c. *Its Impotence* (verse 7)

There is a question to be resolved in connection with the opening of verse 8. Should it be translated, 'For finding fault with it he says to them', or, 'finding fault with them he says'. In view of verse 7 which says, 'if that first covenant had been faultless', we adopt the former alternative.

The idea of 'finding fault' is that of a charge being proved. But what charge could be brought and sustained against the Old Covenant? It is not a charge of any unrighteousness in what it teaches or forbids. Either would reflect on God, its Author. The charge is that it could not give blessing to the disobedient. It could not give life, that is, 'perfect the conscience', as stated in 7:19 and 10:1 (see also *Acts* 15:10 and *Gal.* 3:21). But the blame for this lies in human nature and not in the law, as Romans 8:3–4 makes clear.

d. *Its Impermanence* (verse 13)

Just as the declaration in Jeremiah exposed what the law could not do, so it sounded its death knell. What is more, the announcement sent a shock through the Old Covenant which began an ageing process. The coming of the better, promised, covenant accelerates that decline, and so the Old Covenant is about to disappear, never to be rejuvenated. It has wrinkles all over it, now that the New has come. The destruction of the Temple by the Romans in 70 AD conducted its funeral.

ii. *The character of the New Covenant.*

What distinguishes this is that it was 'enacted on better promises'. This means that what differentiates the New from the Old is, not that it was legally introduced whereas the Old was not, nor that it had promises whereas the Old did not (though it is often thought and taught that the Old was all law and no grace, and the New is all grace and no law), but just that the promises of the New are *better*. This is shown by the words 'not like' in verse 9 and 'new' in verse 13.

First, it is 'not like' the Old Covenant, which people could break and which God could not, therefore, maintain with regard to them. This is what happened, as the words, 'They did not continue in my covenant and I disregarded them', derived from Jeremiah 31:34, make clear. This meant that the promises of the Old were not enjoyed but its curses experienced instead (see below) and that the Babylonian Exile was an act of divine judgement.

Secondly, it is permanent. This is what the word 'new' means. There are two words for 'new' in Greek. One refers to time and means 'recent' or 'novel'. The other refers, not to time, but to what cannot be affected by the passing of time, and therefore cannot change. The adjective used in verse 13 is the latter word. Unlike the first covenant, the second will not age. It cannot do so; it is eternal.

The New is therefore more fully and plainly a covenant of grace than the Old. It cannot be broken and it will not be replaced. That is why its promises are better, and we now turn to a consideration of those.

iii. *The Promises of the Old Covenant.*

The Sinaitic covenant was declared in Exodus 19:1–23:33 and inaugurated in 24:1–18. Its promises are listed in Leviticus 26: 1–13 and also in Deuteronomy 28:1–14. They are related to agricultural productivity and civic security, that is, domestic and national well-being. These are no mean benefits and, though physical in character, they are evidence of the divine favour expressed in Exodus 6:2–8 and 19:4-6.

But these promised blessings were all conditional upon obedience, that is, loyalty to the Lord of the Covenant and all its stipulations, the core of which are the Ten Commandments. If there were disloyalty, then covenant judgements, the exact antithesis of the blessings, would manifest the divine wrath and displeasure (see *Lev.* 26:14–33 and *Deut.* 28:15–68).

iv. *The Promises of the New Covenant.*

These are better than those of the Old in two respects. They are wholly spiritual and they are unconditional.

Verses 10–12 list four spiritual blessings. The first is *regeneration*, and this deals with the reason why people in the Old Testament could not keep the law and so obtain its blessings. They did not have 'a heart', that is an inner disposition and desire, to do so. Writing the law in human hearts deals with that inability. The New Covenant is an internal constraint to obey, whereas the Old was often no more than an external restraint on disobedience. The second, which is *union with God*, actually joins people and God in a bond of loving and mutual devotion. The third is *a knowledge of God*, which is direct fellowship with him and is the possession of each and every one who is regenerated. Fourthly, the basis on which all three blessings are given is *pardon for sin*, which broke Old Covenant fellowship and brought wrath, but which has been dealt with in the New, so that it cannot have the same effect.

These blessings are wonderful in themselves but perhaps the way in which they are given is even more wonderful. Instead of saying, 'And all these blessings shall come upon you . . . if you will obey the LORD your God' (*Deut.* 28:2), we have in verses 10–12, 'I will . . . and they shall'. Instead of 'If you will, then I will', we have 'I will, and you shall'. The former would mean that the blessings would never be ours; the latter, that they certainly will be, and inalienably so.

3. THE MEDIATOR OF THE NEW COVENANT

To conclude this study of the covenants we return to the verse that introduced it, namely verse 6, and to the fact that there is only a better administration because there is a Mediator. Hebrews 7:22 (see comment there) has specified Jesus as a Surety-Mediator, that is, one who not only is a means of revelation, like Moses at Sinai, but is a means of redemption. On Mount Calvary, Jesus procured the blessings of the New Covenant. But he did that because he kept the Old Covenant, and yet bore not only its judgements but that curse which they could only faintly represent. It was in this way that he inaugurated the New – in his own blood.

So the greater blessings which have just been referred to are only provided because of him and what he has done. This is a convenient point to reiterate what lies at the heart of the message of this entire epistle. It is 'the Christ' who makes Christianity different fromevery other religion, Judaism included.

There is in these verses a description, not only of the greater blessings of this better covenant, but also of its universality. In verse 8 there is a reference to the house of Israel and the house of Judah. This is a reflection on the fact that prior to Jeremiah's day the nation had been divided. Even so the New Covenant relates to both, and when it is introduced it will gather in people from north and south, east and west, and make them and others, many others, into a new Israel of God (verse 10).

16

A Greater Sanctuary

Now even the first covenant had regulations of divine worship and the earthly sanctuary. [2] *For there was a tabernacle prepared, the outer one, in which were the lampstand and the table and the sacred bread; this is called the holy place.* [3] *And behind the second veil, there was a tabernacle which is called the Holy of Holies,* [4] *having a golden altar of incense and the ark of the covenant covered on all sides with gold, in which was a golden jar holding the manna, and Aaron's rod which budded, and the tables of the covenant.* [5] *And above it were the cherubim of glory overshadowing the mercy seat; but of these things we cannot now speak in detail.* [6] *Now when these things have been thus prepared, the priests are continually entering the outer tabernacle, performing the divine worship,* [7] *but into the second only the high priest enters, once a year, not without taking blood, which he offers for himself and for the sins of the people committed in ignorance.* [8] *The Holy Spirit is signifying this, that the way into the holy place has not yet been disclosed, while the outer tabernacle is still standing;* [9] *which is a symbol for the time then present, according to which both gifts and sacrifices are offered which cannot make the worshiper perfect in conscience* [10] *since they relate only to food and drink and various washings, regulations for the body imposed until a time of reformation.* [11] *But when Christ appeared as a high priest of the good things to come, He entered through the greater and more perfect tabernacle, not made with hands, that is to say, not of this creation;* [12] *and not through the blood of goats and calves, but through His own blood, He entered the holy place once for all, having obtained eternal redemption* (Heb. 9:1–12).

We have just had a discussion of two covenants, each of which brings into being a community related to God. The 'Old Covenant' created not only a 'holy nation' but also, and primarily, 'a kingdom of priests' (*Exod.* 19:5–6). Israel was to be a worshipping community, having access to God. She was therefore provided with a place in which to worship her covenant Sovereign, and directions as to how to do so. There was an 'earthly sanctuary' and 'regulations of divine worship' (verse 1). Down through her history this pattern was largely preserved, although the place ceased to be a tent (tabernacle) and became a temple that was destroyed and rebuilt more than once, and there was also a period in which sacrifices were suspended. At the time when the letter was written there was a temple in which sacrifices were being offered (verse 6).

By contrast, the 'New Covenant' creates an international church which has no central earthly shrine. Verses 10 and 11 make clear that because 'the great high priest has come' a 'reformation' of the old has occurred, and, as part of this, there is a 'greater and more perfect tabernacle'. What is this 'tabernacle' and what kind of worship is offered there?

The first ten verses of this section describe the old sanctuary and its services, pointing out what should have been learned from it all by those who engaged in such worship. Verses 11 and 12 describe the greater tabernacle and something of the worship that takes place there. More is said on the latter in 10:1–2, 19–25 and 12:18–13:25.

1. THE EARTHLY SANCTUARY AND ITS SERVICES (verses 1–10)
The sanctuary is described in verses 2–5 by way of a reference to its two main parts, the outer tent and the Holy of Holies, and by a list of the items of sacred furniture for each. Directions for their construction had been given by God to Moses (*Exod.* 25:1–31:11) which were carried out exactly (*Exod.* 36:1–40:38)

A question arises in connection with verse 4, where the altar is connected with the ark, and both are introduced after the writer has finished describing the outer court in verse 2. The problem is that the altar was to be placed *outside* the veil (*Exod.* 27:1), whereas the ark was to be placed behind it. The solution to this is to be found by noting that the writer uses the word 'having' in verse 4 and not 'in which' as in verse 2. What he wants to do is to show the connection between what went on at the altar and what was behind the veil, rather than to define their precise locations.

Concerning the items of furniture listed he says, 'of these things we cannot now speak in detail' (verse 5). This aside is interesting and instructive. It indicates that the writer could have said something about the significance of each item from a Christian standpoint, but that he chose not to do so for some reason. This means that all these items had typological significance, and this points to the possibility of there being more types in the Old Testament than are actually identified as such in the New.

How then can we find these types with accuracy? Recall the discussion of 7:1–10 at this point. The answer is that each of these pieces of furniture had a symbolic significance in Israel's worship, one that was specified by God in the word which authorized them. That significance concerns what was being typified in the higher realm.

This is what is stressed in verse 9. There the writer uses the term 'parable', and that means something that is represented by something else. To be coupled with this word are the terms 'example' and 'shadow', found in chapter 8:5. Taken together they mean that persons, objects, events and so on in the Old Testament represent the higher truths and glories of the Christian system, and that they do so by what they signify in their own time and place.

The services are described in summary form in verses 6 and 7, from the daily duties of the priests to the events on the annual Day of Atonement. Here lies the reason, perhaps, why the writer did not present the significance of each piece of furniture found in the outer court and the Holy of Holies. It was because he wanted to draw his readers' attention to what actually went on in the sanctuary and not to the sanctuary itself, so that he might highlight what did not, and could not, go on there. Verses 8–10 begin to indicate that.

There are two further questions to settle with regard to verses 6–10. The first is, What is meant by the 'first tabernacle' in verse 8? Is it the entire sanctuary, or just the outer court as in verses 2 and 6? This study adopts the latter identification, and does so for two reasons. First, while it would not be difficult to argue for a change of reference between verse 2 and verse 8, because so much has intervened, it is very difficult to argue for one between verses 6 and 7 (which make one statement) and verse 8. To assume a continuation of the same meaning is much more natural. Secondly, the words 'still standing' in verse 8 are relevant to this question. They mean more than 'still existing'. 'Still has a standing' is a better rendering, meaning 'still has divine validity'. It is the demarcation of the outer court by God as an area distinct from the most holy place that is in view. That divine validity was withdrawn by the rending of the veil at the time of the Lord's death.

The second question is a more important matter to settle because the uncertainty over whether 'the first tabernacle' is the whole temple or just the outer court does not affect the larger point being made in this section, which is that of what period of time the writer was speaking of in verses 8–10. The writer says that the Spirit was 'showing' (present tense) certain things by the tabernacle and all that went on there. To whom was he doing that, and when? Was it to Christians (post-Calvary and post-Pentecost) or was it to Israelites or Jews (post-Sinai and pre-Calvary?)

The fact that the writer uses the present tense 'signifying' in verse 8 does not have to mean that he was thinking of his own day because he links what he says to the period 'while the first tabernacle [had a] standing'. It could be a way of describing graphically what went on from the time of Moses right up to 'the time of reformation', which is the same as 'the present time' in verse 9. It is the era of the Old Covenant.

The Holy Spirit therefore was teaching something by means of the earthly sanctuary and its services as long as they had divine validity. The implication is that the moment that validity was withdrawn, which took place when the outer court and the Holy of Holies became one area through the rending of the veil at the death of Christ, lesson time was concluded. The Spirit teaches by types, but only up to the era of fulfilment. Then his ministry is linked with what is 'greater and more perfect'.

What was the Holy Spirit teaching? He has been referred to before as speaking Old Testament Scripture (3:7–11; see also 10:15–17), and now he is said to have been 'signifying' something by the very layout and services of the earthly sanctuary. What was it? The answer is 'that the way into the Holiest was not yet made manifest'. This lesson is a positive, not a negative, one. It is not that there is no way into the Holiest. That could not be, because once a year one man went there. It is that the way was not yet opened wide and for all – but that it would be. Meanwhile a worship which was imperfect (verse 9) and could not cleanse (see 7:11, 19 and 10:1–3); which was imposed (verse 10), was required in law (see 7:11–12) and was impermanent (verse 10 - 'until') was in place. It therefore conveyed information about a better time to come, fuelling a longing for it in the minds and hearts of those who saw the messianic age from a distance (11:13). It could not take away sin and yet it commanded obedience. It was the only system of ritual God ever appointed and he deliberately made it unable to save.

While the sacrificial system did not ever have within itself the power to cleanse the defiled conscience of the sinner (verses 9–10), it pointed daily and annually, throughout its long history, to what did. This shows how blind people were to the glory of the Messiah in the Old Testament period and in the time when this letter was written. Sadly, it is still the case (*2 Cor.* 3:14), but 'when it shall turn to the Lord the veil shall be taken away'.

2. THE HEAVENLY SANCTUARY AND ITS SERVICES (verses 11–12)

What these verses describe is encapsulated in the striking phrase 'a time of reformation' in verse 10. The word for 'reformation' is not used anywhere else in the New Testament. It is a compound term meaning 'through' and 'straight' and describes the idea of reconstruction in the interests of improvement. The 'regeneration' in Matthew 19:28 and the 'restitution of all things' in Acts 3:21 are parallel terms and ideas. Using what has been said of the old covenant in these verses as a foil for thought, we would be justified in thinking of this new order as one characterized by perfection (cleansing), liberty and permanence – 'the good things' which have come in Jesus.

The coming of Jesus, the Messiah, introduced an immense change - so great that it seemed more like a revolution than a reformation. To those whose eyes were not opened to the fact that the new was a fulfilment of the old, it certainly seemed so. To unbelieving Jews who thought that the Sinaitic covenant was eternal, Christianity was bound to appear novel. But so great was the change that even believing Jews had difficulty with it. The classic example of this is the apostle Peter, no less, and his reaction to Cornelius on the one hand (see *Acts* 10:15, 44–45; 11:1–18, 19–20) and to the Christian Jews who came to Antioch on the other (see *Acts* 15:1–2; *Gal.* 2:11–21). It was the first major threat in the church, necessitating the council at Jerusalem (*Acts* 15:1–2 and 3–29) in order to prevent a breach in fellowship between Jewish and Gentile Christians. It continued to be a problem, as Romans 14 and 15 indicate.

As the change-over from old to new was as if a new world was being made (see 12:26–27), there was bound to be a new sanctuary. What is this? It has already been described as 'the true tent' (8:2), that is, the real one where God resides, and now it is further termed 'greater and more perfect'. But what is it? We need to note that these verses speak of the Lord as having gone through this tent into heaven. Thinking of this in a literalistic way, like the difference between the outer court and the Holy Place, several views have been advanced about it, namely, that it is the Lord's body, the church, or the physical skies. In our view the first of these interpretations is more substantial than the other two, but the expression 'not made with hands', which means what is not included in Genesis 1:1–2:3, militates against all three. We favour another identification, one based on the tent-holy place reference being metaphorical. Chapter 9:24 indicates that the tent is heaven and, although the adjective 'heavenly' is not used with reference to the 'greater tabernacle', it must be understood in order to set up an effective contrast with what has been said about the 'earthly' tent. Good things have come and are to come because, having offered his own blood as a sacrifice for sin, the High Priest has obtained eternal redemption (see 5:9). Through him heaven has come down to earth and his people worship in him.

17

A Better Sacrifice

[13] For if the blood of goats and bulls and the ashes of a heifer sprinkling those who have been defiled, sanctify for the cleansing of the flesh, [14] how much more will the blood of Christ, who through the eternal Spirit offered Himself without blemish to God, cleanse your conscience from dead works to serve the living God? [15] And for this reason He is the mediator of a new covenant, in order that since a death has taken place for the redemption of the transgressions that were committed under the first covenant, those who have been called may receive the promise of the eternal inheritance. [16] For where a covenant is, there must of necessity be the death of the one who made it. [17] For a covenant is valid only when men are dead, for it is never in force while the one who made it lives. [18] Therefore even the first covenant was not inaugurated without blood. [19] For when every commandment had been spoken by Moses to all the people according to the Law, he took the blood of the calves and the goats, with water and scarlet wool and hyssop, and sprinkled both the book itself and all the people, [20] saying, 'This is the blood of the covenant which God commanded you.' [21] And in the same way he sprinkled both the tabernacle and all the vessels of the ministry with the blood. [22] And according to the Law, one may almost say, all things are cleansed with blood, and without shedding of blood there is no forgiveness. [23] Therefore it was necessary for the copies of the things in the heavens to be cleansed with these, but the heavenly things themselves with better sacrifices than these. [24] For Christ did not enter a holy place made with hands, a mere copy of the true one, but into heaven itself, now to appear in the presence of God

for us; [25] nor was it that He should offer Himself often, as the high priest enters the holy place year by year with blood not his own. [26] Otherwise, He would have needed to suffer often since the foundation of the world; but now once at the consummation He has been manifested to put away sin by the sacrifice of Himself. [27] And inasmuch as it is appointed for men to die once, and after this comes judgment; [28] so Christ also, having been offered once to bear the sins of many, shall appear a second time, not to bear sin, to those who eagerly await Him, for salvation (Heb. 9:13–28).

Sacrifices were offered in the tabernacle as part of the worship of God and so it is not surprising that the author's thought moves from 'the greater tabernacle' to 'better sacrifices'. The transition from the one to the other seems to occur in connection with the words 'his own blood' in verse 12, but, as that verse contrasts with verse 11 where the writer refers to 'the blood of bulls and goats', we will begin this study with verse 13 rather than disturb that balance.

Our aim in this study is to focus attention on the uniqueness of the sacrifice of Christ. Three aspects are presented by the writer. They are: *the greater efficacy of the death of Christ* (verses 13–14), *its absolute necessity* (verses 15–23), and *its unrepeatable finality* (verses 24–28). That is the outline that we will follow but first we must consider what is meant by the term 'blood' as it is basic to everything.

This is a metaphorical term. It is therefore to be thought of in terms of what it symbolizes and not what it is in itself. That this is so is shown by the way in which two other terms are used as synonyms for it in this section, namely 'death' in verse 15 and 'sacrifice' in verse 26. 'Blood' means sacrificial death, that is, a life that is terminated as a punishment for sin at the requirement of God. The crucial Old Testament text on this point is Leviticus 17:11, 'For the life of the flesh is in the blood, and I have given it to you upon the altar to make atonement for your souls: for it is the blood that makes atonement for the soul (NKJV).'

There are three complementary implications to that statement. The first is that blood not shed is the same as a live animal. The second is that blood on the altar is that life ended by death and offered to God, but as something 'given' that is provided by God 'to atone [pay] . . . for sin'. The third is that 'for the soul' is better rendered 'in place of, or at the price of, the life', that is, for the life of the worshipper which is liable to the wrath of God on account of his sin. 'Blood' is therefore a shorthand term for atonement through substitution. It means deliverance from sin's curse and acceptance by God by means of a life offered to God in a penal death. We now take up the three aspects outlined earlier.

1. GREATER EFFICACY (verses 13–14)

'For if . . . how much more': This is another use of the argument from the lesser to the greater, which the writer is fond of because it stresses both certainty and intensity (see 2:2–3; 3:3; 10:28–29; and 12:25). What he wants to highlight by its use at this point is that, although the effect of the blood of Christ is so much greater than that of bulls and goats, it is no less certain.

The fact that each sacrifice is said to have some effect highlights the important truth that no sacrifice that God appoints is destitute of power. Each death does something. But only what it was appointed to do and was suitable to do – no more, and no less. The blood of bulls and goats can and does cleanse physically and socially, but the other cleanses inwardly (the conscience) and makes people servants of the living God. How is that so? It is because that other sacrifice is the death 'of Christ, who through the eternal spirit offered himself without spot to God'. These wonderful words point to something profound and crucial.

Before we examine them, let us notice that verse 13 summarizes the whole of Old Testament sacrificial ritual. It relates to the Day of Atonement and other occasions when a bull or a goat might have been sacrificed (see Leviticus 16 and chapters 1–7), and also to the red heifer offering (see Numbers 19) which was a cleansing rite for physical defilement which excluded Israelites from the camp. Old Testament ritual therefore contained the power to cleanse physical uncleanness and to restore communal fellowship.

Setting those effects alongside that of the death of Christ highlights the difference in kind between the sacrifices and shows that one is indeed 'better' than all the others (see verse 23). We turn now to the sacrifice of Christ which is incomparable and examine the words already quoted from verse 14. There are several elements to isolate and consider, and they are as follows:

i. *'The blood of Christ'.*
This expression points by implication to the difference between an animal and a human, and specifically it identifies that human as the 'Messiah', God's anointed Saviour. 'Christ' is not a surname but an official title, and so his death must have a central place within the saving purpose of God.

ii. *'Through the eternal spirit'*
These words come first in this crucially important clause and they relate to all that follows. We will just mention them in connection with each part of it before advocating a particular understanding of them.

iii. *'He offered . . . to God . . . through the eternal spirit'*
This describes an action. It is often forgotten that Christ was active on Calvary. Though he suffered at the hands of men, the devil, and God, and meekly submitted to all, he was not inactive as bulls and goats were. These words describe how he was active, what he was doing on the cross. He was making an offering to God (see 5:1–3). His priestly ministry is therefore not to be located in heaven alone. Golgotha was an altar and not just a gibbet, because Christ was acting as a priest there. As the old priests were to bring the sacrifice to the Lord symbolically, sprinkling blood on the altar, Christ offered sacrifice to God actually. He did not offer to Satan but to God and 'through the eternal spirit' discloses how that was done.

iii. *'Himself . . . without spot . . . through the eternal spirit'*
Just as a high priest who does not act toward God cannot be a priest, so a priest cannot officiate without a sacrifice (see 8:3). *'Himself . . . without spot'* is therefore a description of the sacrifice which Christ offered. It has two aspects. 'Himself' refers to his humanity and 'without spot' to his perfected obedience. The sacrifice is therefore not that of the sinlessness of the eternal Son, but the righteousness of the incarnate Son, acquired by obedience.

The 'place of a skull' (Golgotha) was a place of sacrifice and the sacrifice was the righteous human self of Jesus. He put himself without sin as a guilt-offering into the hands of a holy God. It was 'through the eternal spirit' that he did that.

iv. *Through (the) eternal spirit*

So far we have skirted around this expression, but hopefully an idea of the immensity of what it refers to has been gained. These words explain how such a sacrifice could be offered on earth to God personally. They are like the fire on the altar that consumed all the burnt offering. But what do they actually refer to?

There are two interpretations and there is something to be said for each of them. The first sees these words as referring to the Lord's divine nature. In favour of this is the fact that there is no definite article before the words 'eternal spirit', and also the fact that the expression 'eternal spirit' resembles what is said in 7:16 about the deity of Jesus. This view yields the meaning that though the humanity of Jesus was without sin, it was infirm and needed the support of his deity. Where was that more necessary than at the cross?

But secondly, there is the view that sees here a reference to the Holy Spirit, and that is what we favour. The omission of the article and the use of the adjective 'eternal' in 7:16 are not decisive considerations against this ('the Spirit' often lacks the article, and 'eternal' is also used of 'inheritance' in 9:15). In favour of understanding 'eternal spirit' as the Holy Spirit is the fact that it is 'Christ' not 'Jesus' that is being spoken of, that is, the Messiah, not just a human, and all that the Messiah did he did by virtue of the Spirit abiding on him. Taking this view yields the wonderful truth that each person of the Holy Trinity was present and active in the moments in which redemption was actually secured, each in his own way. The Father was smiting the Son; the Son was submitting to the Father, and the Spirit was sustaining the incarnate Son. Only a triune God can save!

2. ABSOLUTE NECESSITY (verses 15–23)

When anything is declared to be necessary, there are reasons or circumstances why that is so. This applies to what is said here regarding the sacrifice of Christ. It is required in order that a covenant might be put into operation (verse 18) and that people might be cleansed so as to receive its heavenly benefits (verse 22). We will consider each of these by way of a discussion of a translation difficulty in some of these verses.

The question is whether the word 'testament' should be used in verses 16 and 17 instead of 'covenant' as in verse 15 and verses 18 and 20. There is a real disagreement on this among orthodox scholars and also in Bible translations. The Greek word may be rendered in either way. The NASB uses 'covenant' throughout, but we favour the use of 'testament' or 'last will' for verses 16 and 17 because they contain several legal terms. These are *'be'* in verse 16, which means 'to be brought as evidence', *'in force after men are dead'* and *'no power (validity) at all'*. Quite clearly, the reference here is to the actual disposition of a person's estate as a result of his death.

That being so, it may be questioned whether the word 'testament' should not be used throughout this section. The answer to that is 'No', because the culture reflected in verses 15, 18 and 20 is that of the Old Testament in which a 'last will and testament' arrangement for inheritance was unknown. What is more, to think of the 'first covenant' as a testament would involve the idea of the death of the one who made it, that is God! We therefore need the word 'covenant' in this passage whenever the Old Testament situation is being referred to.

How then can the writer combine these two arrangements in what he says here? He does so because a death was necessary in each, and that is his main point in this section. In the Old Testament world, death is the punishment due when a covenant is broken; in the classical world, a will cannot be put into effect except on the proven death of the testator. Each analogy stresses that the death of Jesus Christ is necessary. On the one hand, without a death, every sinner would have to bear the curse of his disobedience, and on the other, no sinner would inherit a blessing.

But there may well be a deeper level of truth in these verses, one that not only does justice to the two kinds of death just mentioned but also binds them together. It is that in the Old Testament the Covenant-Maker intimates that he himself would take the place of covenant-breakers so that the blessings of the covenant would become their inheritance. This is seen in Genesis 15, where God passes between the pieces of the animals, invoking upon himself the judgment if it should be infringed. That is what actually happened when Jesus Christ died, as he declared with reference to the cup in the Upper Room. Jesus Christ's death therefore takes the place of sinners who have broken the covenant.

The writer is therefore combining both worlds – past and present – to stress that the sacrifice of Christ was essential. He does allude to the idea of a last will, but his 'world view' is that of 'covenant', as verses 18 to 23 make clear.

3. UNREPEATABLE FINALITY (verses 24–28)

In these verses there is a contrast between 'often' in verses 25 and 26 and 'once', which means 'once-for-all', in verses 26 to 28. Repetition characterized the ministrations of the old priests. They offered sacrifices, went behind the veil and then reappeared, only to repeat the whole process year after year. Though Christ is in heaven, hidden from earthly view in a way that resembles the high priest's being obscured by the temple veil, he will not reappear to deal with sin again. He is in heaven in a once-for-all manner for his people and will come again to receive them only because he has 'put away sin by the sacrifice of himself'.

It is just not possible for him to die again. The writer combines several lines of thought to demonstrate how ridiculous this notion is. He was in earnest on this point because of the Jewish threat to the finality of Christ's sacrifice. What does he say?

First, death is unrepeatable – whoever's death it is. Verse 27 makes that point with regard to every human being and the same applied to Christ by definition. Apart from the wholly exceptional cases recorded in the Bible (*2 Kings* 4:34; *Luke* 7:14 and 8:53; *John* 11:43 and *Acts* 9:40), people do not die physically twice.

Secondly, Christ had to be 'manifested' in order to die, that is, he had to be born and become incarnate. That could only happen once. In order for him to 'die again' he has to be born once again.

Thirdly, the death he died was at a particular time in God's purpose. It was 'at the end of the ages', that is, at the end of the old era and the beginning of the new. That moment in history cannot be repeated. Man's clock can be turned back, but God's cannot be. In this case they both tell the same time.

Fourthly, he could not offer for sin without suffering for sin. The change from 'offer' in verse 25 to 'suffer' in verse 26 is of the utmost importance. The writer is using a form of argument known as *reductio ad absurdum* at this point. He says that, if Christ's death did not deal with all sin, then not only would he need to suffer again and therefore live again, but he would have to live before he was born, in order to suffer for sins committed during that period.

It is just not possible to offer for sin so as to take it away without suffering on account of it, and that means one death. It is this that cuts decisively against the notion that in the Mass the church re-presents Christ to the Father as a sacrifice for ongoing sin. If that were necessary, because of our sins committed after Calvary, there would have to be a Calvary every day, and that means an incarnation every day, a BC/AD every day – an endless replay of history! To offer oneself in suffering once is enough for all time. More than that, it is enough for the endless ages of eternity!

18

Perfected for Ever

For the Law, since it has only a shadow of the good things to come and not the very form of things, can never by the same sacrifices year by year, which they offer continually, make perfect those who draw near. *2* Otherwise, would they not have ceased to be offered, because the worshipers having once been cleansed, would no longer have had consciousness of sins? *3* But in those sacrifices there is a reminder of sins year by year. *4* For it is impossible for the blood of bulls and goats to take away sins. *5* Therefore, when He comes into the world, He says, 'Sacrifice and offering Thou hast not desired, but a body Thou hast prepared for Me; *6* in whole burnt offerings and sacrifices for sin Thou hast taken no pleasure. *7* Then I said, "Behold, I have come (in the roll of the book it is written of Me) to do Thy will, O God."' *8* After saying above, 'Sacrifices and offerings and whole burnt offerings and sacrifices for sin Thou hast not desired, nor hast Thou taken pleasure in them (which are offered according to the Law), *9* then He said, 'Behold I have come to do Thy will.' He takes away the first in order to establish the second. *10* By this will we have been sanctified through the offering of the body of Jesus Christ once for all. *11* And every priest stands daily ministering and offering time after time the same sacrifices, which can never take away sins; *12* but He, having offered one sacrifice for sins for all time, sat down at the right hand of God, *13* waiting from that time onward until His enemies be made a footstool for His feet. *14* For by one offering He has perfected for all time those who are sanctified. *15* And the Holy Spirit also bears witness to us; for after saying, *16* 'This is the covenant that I will make with them after those days, says the Lord: I will put My

*laws upon their heart, and upon their mind I will write them,'
He then says, [17] 'And their sins and their lawless deeds I will
remember no more.' [18] Now where there is forgiveness of these
things, there is no longer any offering for sin* (Heb. 10:1–18).

As these verses conclude the section of this letter which describes
what is special about the High Priesthood of the Lord Jesus
Christ, it is not surprising that they contain some teaching which
has been mentioned before. Two such truths are the inadequacy of
the Sinaitic ritual and the Aaronic priesthood to take away sins
(verses 1–4) and the ability of Jesus Christ to do so by his death (verse
10). Verses 11–13 state these points crisply.

It would, however, be a great mistake to regard these verses as
repetition and so to pass them over. Holy Scripture does not contain
any 'padding', that is, monotonous and purposeless repetition. When
an 'old' truth is being presented, some new light is always cast on it
either by way of more detail being given about it or by means of a
connection made between it and something else. Sometimes a minor
theme in one passage becomes a major one in another, and that is
the case here.

In these verses what is to the fore is not so much 'priest' or
'sacrifice', but 'worshippers' (see verses 1–3, 10, 11, 14, 15–17 and 18).
Although they have been mentioned before, for example in 9:9 and
9:14, they are here highlighted in terms of the effect of the 'once-
for-all sacrifice' of 'the great high priest' on them. We will therefore
consider these verses from that standpoint, raising some questions
about the concept of no longer having 'consciousness of sins' in
verse 2.

1. WHAT IS 'CONSCIOUSNESS OF SIN'?
Consciousness necessarily implies an awareness; it is something
internal. No longer having 'consciousness of sins' therefore means
that an awareness of sins has been dispelled. This does not mean that
a worshipper becomes oblivious of sin's existence in the world or of
its presence and effects in himself (see *1 John* 1:8, 10). It is a particular
kind of 'consciousness' that is being referred to.

The word the writer uses here is also used in 9:14 and 10:22 where
it is translated 'conscience'. One has only to mention the word

'conscience' in connection with 'sins' for the adjective 'guilty' to spring to mind, and that is the kind of 'consciousness' which is in view. It is an accusing conscience, an uneasy awareness of sins having been committed, which are as yet unforgiven (*Rom.* 2:14–16). While this is something which, to a degree, is a universal reality (*Rom.* 1:32) it can become particularly accentuated in those with a heightened awareness of law, as those described here.

There are variants of this expression 'no longer having consciousness of sins' in other verses of this section. Verse 2 speaks of 'having been purged', verse 10 of 'having been sanctified' and verse 14 of 'having been perfected for ever'. All these verbs are in a Greek tense which describes something as having been accomplished in the past, with effects continuing into the present. A decisive and lasting *inward* change is therefore what is being spoken of as the effect of the death of Christ. In previous chapters the emphasis has been on the God-ward direction of his death, here it is on the man-ward result. While the former is primary, as sin is against God, the latter is essential too, and vital for the sinner laden with guilt. We therefore change focus from the objective and God-ward realm in chapter 9 to the subjective and man-ward in chapter 10. This amounts to the forgiveness spoken of in verse 18.

2. WHAT CANNOT TAKE AWAY SINS, AND WHY NOT?

The answer to this first question is in verse 1. It is all the sacrifices which are prescribed by the law, whether offered annually on the Day of Atonement (verse 10) or daily (verse 11). The writer is emphatic on this point, doubly so. In verse 1 he writes that they 'can never' take away sins and that includes any time in the past as well as the present or the future. They could not do so when they were brand new, they cannot at the time of writing and will not, however many times they are offered. But in addition to this blanket denial, there is an absolute prohibition on the point in verse 4, by the words, 'It is impossible'. It is no more likely that an animal sacrifice will one day take away sin than it is that God will tell a lie (6:18). There is an underlying reason for this (see below).

This total failure is illustrated by the fact that the sacrifices had continued to be, and were still being, offered (verses 1, 2, 3 and 11). They were powerful to remind people of their sins but powerless to remove them from the conscience. That was particularly emphasized on the Day of Atonement when all the sins of the whole preceding year were called to mind and confessed. But the extensive scope of the ritual lacked a commensurate effect. It did not actually cleanse the sinner: if it had, it would not have been repeated – once.

The Hebrews are therefore not to think that what was going on in the Temple ritual showed up what they lacked. Rather, its repetition showed that their fellow Jews did not have what they had (13:9–10).

But secondly, why were (and are) such sacrifices deficient? There is a twofold reason given: first, in verse 1, *the kind of administration to which the sacrifices belonged;* second, in verse 4, *the nature of the sacrifices themselves.* We shall consider each in turn.

i. Although the sacrifices in view were not determined by human convention or regulation but by divine law or appointment, *that arrangement itself was a shadow cast by a brilliant reality and not the reality itself.* It did not contain 'the good things to come' (9:11; see comment on that verse and on 8:6); it could only represent them. The ceremonial system did not have redemptive virtue with which to invest the sacrifices. A signpost has value to a traveller but it is not the same as being at home with a meal on the table.

ii. There was *a glaring disproportion between the sacrifice and the worshipper;* the difference between an animal and a human being. A bull or a goat can illustrate something to a human being but can never actually take his place. Another human may, in certain circumstances, but no animal can, because action by instinct, or even response to a stick or carrot, is a world away from heart-felt and energetic obedience (9:13–14).

3. WHAT CAN TAKE AWAY SINS, AND WHY?
It is 'the offering of the body of Jesus Christ'. The introduction of the word 'body' in verses 5–10 is significant. It stands in contrast to the word 'blood' in verse 4, but this does not mean that the death of Jesus is not a blood-sacrifice. That is not the point of the contrast. The writer is not speaking of the sacrifice of a body as distinct from blood, in the sense of the giving up or laying down of a life, but of

the taking of a body so that it might be obediently offered up in a blood-sacrifice to God. The idea that the death of Christ is the release of the virtue of his life in the world in order that others might be influenced to a like self-sacrifice is not what is being taught here. Again the writer uses the verb 'offer', which he has used of levitical sacrifices and of Jesus Christ and, as is shown in 9:25–26, it is not possible to offer for sin without suffering its penalty, which is death. In any case verse 12, 'having offered one sacrifice for sins for ever', is explicit on this point.

The introduction of the word 'body', and the stress placed upon it, are to emphasize the necessity and the reality of human-ness and obedience. That is the key to the efficacy of the Lord's death for human sinners – a life in human flesh and blood had to be lived, and that life had to die.

The way in which this is emphasized here is important to notice. Once more, it is by way of a use of an Old Testament text, in this case Psalm 40. But there are two distinct features to note. First, the writer uses the quoted material twice, giving the quotation in verses 5–7 in the past tense, and interpreting it in the present in verses 8–9. This points to the importance of the Psalm text to the argument that is being developed. But secondly, and even more strikingly, the Old Testament text is put in the mouth of Jesus and is made contemporaneous with his coming. As a result, Psalm 40 does not describe what the writer to the Hebrews thought about his coming, but what Jesus thought about it as he came.

What is that? It is the inadequacy of the levitical sacrifices and ministry. The writer adds the words 'which are offered according to the law', as he argues from the text. David had summarized all sorts of levitical sacrifices (sacrifice, offering, burnt-offering and sin-offering) and wrote that they were not desired by God as an alternative to the heart and life sacrifice of the worshipper. They were God's appointed ways for expressing worshipful obedience. David therefore resolved to give to God that which he desired, and to do so in the body that God had given to him. So did 'great David's greater Son'– even more so. Sacrifices by themselves were unable to pardon, and if the Son had not become incarnate, God's will would never have been perfectly done and so there would never have been cleansing for guilty sinners.

But that is what he came to do, and did. The word 'Behold' at the beginning of verses 7 and 9 indicates how amazing, even how miraculous it was that the righteous, offended God, who demanded obedience as a condition of pardon for rebels, should himself provide it *via* the body and blood of his own Son! It is because the law of God was perfectly done that the sacrifice was both sufficient and effective for ever. It has the virtue to perfect the conscience before God and also to continue to sanctify (verse 14).

4. But How Can Worshippers Know This?
We have said that the main emphasis in this passage is on the conscious state of worshippers. There is therefore one question left to consider, and it is how a worshipper can know, as really as he knew guilt, that he is freely and fully pardoned. God knows that his law has been kept by his Son and that he can ask no more. He has consequently enthroned him at his right hand. The Son is seated there, knowing that no more can be asked of him and his universal triumph is sure (verses 12 and 13). But how can the sinner be as sure as that of having been pardoned and accepted? Can he?

The answer lies in the promise of the New Covenant, found in Jeremiah 31:33 and already quoted in Chapter 8. But it is not reproduced here as it is there. For one thing the item which speaks about 'knowing the Lord' is omitted; but more importantly, the quotation is introduced differently. In Hebrews 8 it is prefaced by 'he' or 'it says'. Here, it is, 'The Holy Spirit bears witness to us'. That solemn verb, its present tense, and the words *'to us'*, refer to the ministry of the Holy Spirit as he speaks in the heart the given and recorded Word of God. What is more, to the opening words, 'After saying', must be added something like, 'He then says', and then comes the promise that God will not remember the sins of which the worshipper is aware. He will never remind the worshipper of them. That promise, given formally by the Spirit, once in Jeremiah and once in Hebrews, is spoken by him again in the troubled conscience, and pacifies it. Where such forgiveness is given, there is no need for further sacrifice and the worshipper knows it. The burdened sinner becomes a willing servant – for ever.

PART 3

Persevering Faith
(10:19 – 13:25)

The old saying, 'Strike while the iron is hot', is a good rule for preachers to follow. As we have seen, our writing-preacher does this, following up his teaching with calls to action. As a result his whole letter becomes an address to people, as all sermons should be. People should be aware that they are being spoken to from beginning to end.

Even so, this letter does end with a lengthy pastoral address. But, unlike many sermons, this one is not an anti-climax. It drives home the message of the letter in a number of ways, and it may be useful at the outset to draw attention to four of its features.

1. *Its basis is that, since a 'better' religion than Judaism has been described in this letter, a better kind of life is appropriate.* Just as living in the Old Covenant was to be expressed by keeping its laws, so life in the New Covenant is to be expressed in conformity with the writer's inspired words, as he interprets those requirements and applies them.

2. *Though the message is intended for a local congregation, the writer uses the second person plural.* His 'sermon' is therefore directed to each, as to all; to individuals, and not just to the corporate entity.

3. *It contains admonition and not only encouragement,* because there are sins and dangers to be dealt with, and these are not to be minimized. Christian preaching is therefore not to be just positive, although it should always hold out hope.

4. *It encompasses a range of relationships, in the church, in the family and in society at large.* The Hebrews have come to 'the heavenly Jerusalem' and received 'a kingdom that cannot be shaken' (see 12:22 and 28). They are therefore to 'serve God acceptably with reverence and godly fear'. So should we.

19

Keep On Believing

Since therefore, brethren, we have confidence to enter the holy place by the blood of Jesus, ²⁰ by a new and living way which He inaugurated for us through the veil, that is, His flesh, ²¹ and since we have a great priest over the house of God, ²² let us draw near with a sincere heart in full assurance of faith, having our hearts sprinkled clean from an evil conscience and our body washed with pure water. ²³ Let us hold fast the confession of our hope without wavering, for He who promised is faithful; ²⁴ and let us consider how to stimulate one another to love and good deeds, ²⁵ not forsaking our own assembling together, as is the habit of some, but encouraging one another; and all the more, as you see the day drawing near. ²⁶ For if we go on sinning willfully after receiving the knowledge of the truth, there no longer remains a sacrifice for sins, ²⁷ but a certain terrifying expectation of judgment, and the fury of a fire which will consume the adversaries. ²⁸ Anyone who has set aside the Law of Moses dies without mercy on the testimony of two or three witnesses. ²⁹ How much severer punishment do you think he will deserve who has trampled under foot the Son of God, and has regarded as unclean the blood of the covenant by which he was sanctified, and has insulted the Spirit of grace? ³⁰ For we know Him who said, 'Vengeance is Mine, I will repay.' And again, 'The Lord will judge His people.' ³¹ It is a terrifying thing to fall into the hands of the living God. ³² But remember the former days, when, after being enlightened, you endured a great conflict of sufferings, ³³ partly, by being made a public spectacle through reproaches and tribulations, and partly by becoming sharers with those who were so treated. ³⁴ For you showed sympathy to the prisoners,

and accepted joyfully the seizure of your property, knowing that
you have for yourselves a better possession and an abiding one.
³⁵ Therefore, do not throw away your confidence, which has a great
reward. ³⁶ For you have need of endurance, so that when you
have done the will of God, you may receive what was promised.
³⁷ For yet in a very little while, He who is coming will come, and
will not delay. ³⁸ But My righteous one shall live by faith; And
if he shrinks back, My soul has no pleasure in him. ³⁹ But we are
not of those who shrink back to destruction, but of those who
have faith to the preserving of the soul (Heb. 10:19–39).

We will try to follow the writer's method as closely as possible
in this section. An important lesson can be learned from it.
First, he summarizes the blessings which are found in Jesus as high
priest (verses 19–21) and states how they should be responded to,
especially in the light of his impending return (verses 22–25). He
then moves on to issue a warning lest the Hebrews should respond
otherwise (verses 26–31), but concludes on a positive note with an
appeal to them to live by faith (verses 32–39). The point to note is
that, although the writer speaks so forcefully to the Hebrews, he still
calls them 'brothers' (verse 19), and the lesson is that professing
Christians are not to be handled roughly, whatever their condition.
This same balanced way of speaking is found in chapter 3:1, in
relation to verses 6 and 12, and in chapter 6:9 in relation to verses
4–6.

1. Blessings, Responses and the Lord's Return

The 'day drawing near' in verse 25 is the personal return of Christ.
It has already been referred to in 9:28 and is again in view in verses
37 and 38. It is all that 'the day of the Lord' means in the Old
Testament, and even more. It is not only the great occasion when
the people of God will be saved by a judgement which will sweep
away God's foes and theirs, just like the Red Sea deliverance, but it
will inaugurate eternity and fix the destinies of those in the world
and in the church. It is therefore an event for which preparation is
appropriate and that is done by way of responding appropriately to
the blessings received.

i. *The Blessings*

Two blessings are specified, but they obviously include many more. They are *ever-open access to God* and *a never-ending headship over the church*. Each of these is bound up with the Lord Jesus Christ. He alone provides access to God and he presides over the church. The words 'we have' indicate the possession of these blessings and not just their availability.

The mention of the veil that barred entry to the Holy of Holies and of the high priest ruling over the worship of the people of God indicate that the provisions of the old system of worship provide the background for an explanation of these blessings. The ritual of the Day of Atonement is therefore a foil for the worship of the church on earth, and in heaven.

Access to God is through the body, or human nature, of Jesus that he offered up in death to God as a sacrifice for sin. The temple veil that was torn from top to bottom, as if by an unseen hand, made it clear that people could enter God's presence with boldness or confidence through him. Two adjectives are used to describe this way. Both could be translated by the one English term 'new', but the first means new from the standpoint of time that is 'recent', the second means 'new' in terms of its quality that is 'permanent'. 'Living' is a good paraphrase of it. This way will always be open and never be closed because the one who died has atoned for sin and is forever alive.

Headship over the house means that Jesus is Lord of the church. He is 'over' his people in the sense that he is their 'head', directing them by his Word and animating them by his Spirit.

ii. *The Responses*

Three of these are specified namely *'drawing near'*, *'holding on'* and *'thinking of others'*, but, like the blessings, they include others. They are all presented in a way ('let us . . .') that calls for a response that is willing and ongoing, not begrudged and fitful, and the writer includes himself in his exhortations.

First, they are to 'draw near' to God, more often than daily, realizing that they are in the sanctuary of his presence where they will receive mercy and grace through the Mediator. This is to be done with sincerity as well as confidence, with 'clean hands and a pure heart', in a spirit which answers to the way the high priest prepared to enter the Holy of Holies by means of blood and water (*Lev.* 16: 3–5).

Secondly, they are to 'hold fast' to the hope they have confessed and do so without that wavering which had been so evident among them. The fact that God is faithful to his recorded promises should strengthen their faith that they will be provided with what they need in the known present and unknown future.

Thirdly, they are to care for others in the believing community and to help them on in their life of faith. The writer uses the word 'stimulate' or 'exasperate' here to make clear that the kind of help that he is intending is one which does create a reaction – but a good one! Because Christian brothers and sisters are not all the same, having different needs and reacting best to differing approaches, real wisdom is called for in order to be truly helpful and not the reverse. Job and his comforters are not a good example at this point. People are to be helped, but not carried. Love and good works are the order of the day *for* each and all, and *to* each and all.

One way, or setting, in which all this can be done is by 'gathering together'. What is in view here includes all meetings for worship and fellowship, whether on the Lord's day or not. Corporate praise and prayer, the ministry of the Word and mutual edification should be conducted as at the foot of the cross and before the throne, and as if the Lord himself were physically present. To be needlessly absent is to deprive oneself, both of being helped and of helping others, but more seriously of drifting in the direction of danger.

2. WARNING, THE FORMER DAYS AND AN APPEAL

It is worth noting the order in which the writer proceeds at this point. He does not recall the past and then proceed to warn the Hebrews about their present condition. Instead, he warns them *before* recalling the past, so that what was once true about them will have the effect of driving them away from that concerning which he now warns them about. What he says about the 'former days' is therefore an encouraging reminder of what is yet attainable – not what is beyond recall. His outlook is positive.

i. The warning

This warning is more specific and severe than that of 6:4–6 (re-read the discussion of these verses on pp. 57–61). Doubtless this is because of all that has been unfolded in 7:1–10:18. It is more awe-inspiring in two respects: first, in terms of the description given of the sin committed, and, secondly, in terms of the judgement of God upon those who commit it. Once more, and with regard to both, the writer uses the argument from lesser to greater.

The sin is described as 'sinning wilfully after receiving the knowledge of the truth'. These words have often been misunderstood, with great harm and loss resulting to oneself and others in the process. 'Sinning wilfully' is not sinning in spite of what one has been taught and believed. We need to turn to the Old Testament here to understand the expression, as the following verses invite us to do. Numbers 15:22–31 was probably in the author's mind when he wrote these words.

There are two categories of sin in the Old Testament. The first is termed 'sinning unintentionally' (*Num.* 15:22–29; see also *Lev.* 4:2, 27). The Hebrew word means 'error' or 'inadvertence' and it is used of manslaughter in Deuteronomy 19:4. 'Sinning unintentionally' (or 'ignorantly' [NKJV]) is therefore sinning with some lack of awareness of sin's awfulness. Sacrifices were provided for all such sins. This corresponds to our 'sins of omission and commission'.

By contrast, 'sinning wilfully' is described as 'sinning with a raised hand' (*Num.* 15: 30) A 'raised hand' is a feature of oath-making. It therefore expresses solemn intent. Such a sin is like committing first-degree murder, not manslaughter. It is described in Numbers 15:31 as 'despising the word of the LORD'; an act 'with malice aforethought'. There is no sacrifice provided for it in the Old Testament. An example of this is found in Deuteronomy 17:2–7 with reference to blatant idolatry, which is the same as rejection of the entire covenant. Without delay, but not without corroborated testimony, the offender was to be executed and the evil removed.

The New Testament equivalent to all this is far worse. Corresponding to Moses' law are the essentials of the saving gospel, namely Christ's deity, his blood and the gracious Spirit. To despise these, that is, to renounce them, casting scorn on one's previous confession and allegiance to them, is an unspeakable desecration.

The inevitable consequence is described, not just as a most awful punishment handed down, but as a terrifying meeting with the Judge himself, in all his just fury and vengeance. In this way 'it is a fearful thing to fall into' his hands. Because he is a living God, his wrath will never die.

But perhaps the most awful thing about these words is that they are directed not to the unbelieving, blaspheming world but to the 'Hebrews', and therefore to the visible church in every age and to every professing Christian. It is not only the world that God will judge but 'his people' too. There is no other gospel for the church, as well as for the world, and no 'second chance' after death for either.

ii. *The Former Days*

Even so, the writer says, 'if we', in verse 26, and not 'you have'. He can therefore move on to encourage, without diminishing the gravity of his warning. Calling on them not to give up and turn back, he bids them to look back and to look forward, back to their early Christian days and forward to the coming of Christ on the last day.

Looking back, they would remember a time when they had faced difficulties which were far greater than those they were now encountering, and that they had borne up bravely under them. But, what is more, they had done so with a heavenly light in their minds and joy in their hearts. Unmoved by suffering and derision, their concern was to identify themselves with other persecuted believers. They had reckoned their material losses to be as nothing when compared to substantial and permanent gain in heaven. Why should they now throw everything away – when things were easier? Their real problem was their loss of a heavenly perspective. That is what caused their half-heartedness.

iii. *An Appeal*

So he calls them to look forward and upward, reminding them that it would not be long before the Lord returned and their faith and hope would be rewarded. Endurance, the soldier's fortitude, is the mark of those whom God regards as righteous. Keeping on believing is the same as keeping on living. The just shall *live* by faith, as the next chapter makes clear.

20

One People – One Faith

Now faith is the assurance of things hoped for, the conviction of things not seen. ² For by it the men of old gained approval . . . ³⁹ And all these, having gained approval through their faith, did not receive what was promised, ⁴⁰ because God had provided something better for us, so that apart from us they should not be made perfect (Heb. 11:1–2, 39–40).

I t will be noticed that the verses printed above form the beginning and the end of this well-known chapter. They have been isolated because they contain some truths that are important for understanding it as a whole and which often are not appreciated.

In the immediately preceding section, the writer has called on the Hebrews to be like those who 'believe to the saving of the soul'. Who might they be? Here he shows them that there is no lack of such people, even among their own forbears, who are 'a cloud of witnesses' (see 12:1) to them in that regard. They tell and inspire the Hebrews (and us) that 'keeping on believing' is not impossible. That provides the force of this chapter, but its underlying logic is that there is but one people of God, and that the testimony of those who have gone before is relevant to those who succeed them. These are the matters which we will consider.

1. ONE PEOPLE

The people who are referred to in this chapter differed from one and another in terms of time, race and sex, but the fundamental assertion about them is that they were all one. Verses 39 and 40 refer to 'them' and 'us', but affirm that they will not be perfected without us. We will focus attention on two expressions in verses 39 and 40 that point this out.

i. *They 'obtained a good testimony'* (verse 39).

This chapter asserts that believing involves bearing testimony to what is believed. This is done by word and deed, by confessing that one is a 'stranger and a pilgrim on the earth' and living as such (verse 13). But it also involves 'obtaining a testimony' or 'gaining approval', as is made clear in verse 2 and this verse. Whose testimony is this? It is God's. He who does not leave himself without a witness on the earth does not leave his believing people without his witness from heaven. 'He is not ashamed to be called their God', and his ringing endorsement of their faith resounds in Holy Scripture itself, and not only in this chapter. He has placed their sincerity and their endurance on record for generations following. In that sense, all those who have died and whose lives are recorded in Old Testament Scripture speak to those who live in Christian times with the voice of God. That also applies to the New Testament record as well, and, by extension, something similar may be said of those whose names are recorded in the annals of Christian history. They all say, 'Keep on!'

It therefore follows that the Old Testament not only has something to say to Christians about Jesus as the Messiah and the new era he inaugurated, but also about how they themselves should live in it. We have seen a number of times that the writer does the former, identifying Jesus as the Christ of God. But he also does the latter, and here he does so at length.

Sadly, these two ways of understanding and interpreting the Old Testament are often set over against each other and even allowed to cancel each other out. But there is no necessary conflict between them. They are complementary. The same verb 'to testify' (which has God or Scripture as its subject) is used of both. The Old Testament taught the people of God that the Messiah was coming, and how they ought to live because of God's gracious choice and deliverance. The New Testament says that he has come and teaches the same for the same reasons, explaining and augmenting the Old Testament correctly when it does so. Jesus taught his disciples to remember Lot's wife as well as to remember him. 1 Corinthians 10:11 says definitively: 'Now these things happened to them as an example, and they were written for our instruction, upon whom the ends of the ages have come.'

Like the patriarchs and all their believing descendants, we are pilgrims and strangers in this world. Our home is not here. We must be people 'of whom the world [is] not worthy', and 'of whom God is not ashamed', and we need the Old Testament to help us do that.

ii. *'They should not be made perfect apart from us'* (verse 40).

All those who are referred to in this chapter lived in the pre-Christian era. Some lived between the Creation and the Exodus; others between that and the entry into Canaan; still others in the time of the kings and some in the period between Malachi and the birth of Jesus. In making his list it seems as if the writer reflected on the Old Testament from its beginning and began to select whatever suited his purpose. He majored on details from the books of Genesis to Joshua before realizing that he had to hurry and become more selective or his list would be endless. He therefore names some judges, one king and 'the goodly fellowship of the prophets' as a whole, summarizing the exploits of faith of this largely unnamed host. He has the whole of the pre-Christian 'church' in view.

What does this have to say to us? It is that there is a unity among the people of God in both dispensations, BC and AD. This has already been mentioned in 3:1–6 with regard to the 'one house' of God. What is more, this unity is not based on a common nationality, although the recipients of this letter were all 'Hebrews'. The list includes Gentiles too. After all, this list does contain a Canaanite, Rahab.

The chapter makes abundantly clear that the unity is based on a faith which has as its single, and precious, focus, that 'something better' which God promised in Christ. While verses 39 and 40 recognize a distinction between the people of the two eras, it refuses to separate them totally. They had the same promise that Christians have, but we have it in a 'better' form. Even so we will not be 'made perfect' without them, which means to receive all that the promise contains. That will only happen to all the people of God together and it will happen because the church of God is whole and entire. Faith binds believing Jews and Gentiles together. The church is one because the gospel is one. There are not two 'peoples' of God, the Christian church and the Jewish nation, because there are not, and never have been, two gospels. There is but one 'olive tree' (*Rom.* 11:17).

2. ONE FAITH

With that background in mind we can narrow down our focus to what is the main theme of the chapter – faith. We will note and consider two expressions in the first two verses that relate to the nature of faith and its activity, and then pick up what is said about God as the object of faith in verse 6. That will complete the introduction to this great chapter.

i. *The nature of faith – 'Faith is the assurance of things hoped for, the conviction of things not seen'.*

This statement about faith is important, but, contrary to what is often thought and said, it is not a definition of it. There are aspects of faith which it does not include, for example, there is no mention of the Lord Jesus Christ in his death, which is the object of faith, or of repentance, which is faith's inseparable accompaniment. It is rather a description of faith which suits the subject matter that is being treated and the need of those addressed.

It is therefore a key to the chapter and the exhortation which it conveys, describing the kind of faith which the Hebrews have just been urged to cultivate – the faith that keeps on believing and will not give up. Such faith, the preacher says, relates to 'things hoped for', which are, by definition, 'things not seen'. The writer has just referred to the prospect of a 'better possession and an abiding one' in heaven (10:34). He has earlier spoken of that sabbath-rest (4:10) and he will shortly refer to the 'heavenly country [and] city' (11:16).

This faith registers the glorious reality of these things in the believer's soul and generates the certainty of possessing them. It therefore gives an existence to the intangible and an expectation of the invisible – in the heart. This is the faith that will endure. It is informed by a promise from the God who 'is' and who will reward 'those who [continue to] diligently seek him' (verse 6), and is characterized by a 'sight' of him who is invisible (verse 27). The unseen world has, as it were, 'dropped anchor' in the believer's soul (6:19), and life 'within the veil' is a present reality.

ii. *The activity of faith – 'By faith . . .'*

So many verses in this chapter begin with these words. They record deeds of faith, acts done by virtue of its power. This chapter is therefore largely about faith at work. Faith is not some mystical, much less magical, dynamism which operates apart from human activity. 'By faith' is the same as 'through believing', that ordinary but amazing, ongoing and repeated counting on God to be as true and as good as his Word. What we have in Hebrews 11 is a record of what people did, in the trials of life and in the throes of death, through believing the God 'who is' and 'who is a rewarder of those who diligently seek him' (verse 6).

Those two statements about God are foundational. The first, '[God] is', does not just mean that he exists, over against what is notional or fictional. It is the assertion that he ever lives in all the attributes of his eternal Being. The second refers to the good and just way in which he responds to those who seek him. It cannot be vain to trust and serve him.

But the Hebrews were distracted or preoccupied with what was visible – the land, the temple, its services, and the earthly city. They saw all this as through a powerful microscope, whereas the non-visible world was being viewed through the wrong end of a telescope. As a result, they were crippled and weakened in faith. The confidence and endurance that they lacked could only be recovered by an awareness of the reality of the unseen and a conviction of its greater glory. Their forebears (verse 2), that is the 'great cloud of witnesses' (12:1), all had this faith, as the writer goes on to show.

21

Real Believing

³ By faith we understand that the worlds were prepared by the word of God, so that what is seen was not made out of things which are visible. ⁴ By faith Abel offered to God a better sacrifice than Cain, through which he obtained the testimony that he was righteous, God testifying about his gifts, and through faith, though he is dead, he still speaks. ⁵ By faith Enoch was taken up so that he should not see death; and he was not found because God took him up; for he obtained the witness that before his being taken up he was pleasing to God. ⁶ And without faith it is impossible to please Him, for he who comes to God must believe that He is and that He is a rewarder of those who seek Him. ⁷ By faith Noah, being warned by God about things not yet seen, in reverence prepared an ark for the salvation of his household, by which he condemned the world, and became an heir of the righteousness which is according to faith (Heb. 11:3–7).

We have selected these few verses and made them into a section on their own for two reasons. First and foremost, they present a composite picture of what is involved in true believing, and secondly, they relate to Genesis 1–10, a tract of Scripture to which we often do not give the careful attention it merits. Before we begin making our way through the picture gallery of Old Testament believers, we will find, from the earliest period of divine revelation, perhaps to our surprise, a list of the constituent elements of faith.

1. FAITH AND HISTORY

Believing is historical; it takes place on earth, in time and space. These verses refer to the period between the creation of the world and the call of Abram. They make clear that people did believe in those days, and that that period was no less historical than all the ages which followed it. To call that era 'pre-history' because there are no independent and contemporaneous records to Genesis 1–10 is, at the very least, to suspend judgement about the trust-worthiness of Scripture.

These verses, and the chapter as a whole, are full of history, full of accounts of God's words to men and their deeds for God. We have references in them to the two great events in cosmic history prior to Abraham, namely Creation and Flood, and, by necessary implication, to sin's entry into the world, and to Abel, Cain, Enoch and Noah.

Faith and history are not enemies, therefore. There is the closest relationship between them. The Old Testament makes clear time and time again that faith is rooted in history – not 'supra–history', which is but another way of saying 'myth'. This is true in relation to what the New Testament records as well. Believing is not day-dreaming.

2. FAITH AND REASON

We will see that the writer makes this point in verse 3, although in some respects what he says there sounds strange, coming as it does after verses 1 and 2. The writer has referred to the faith of 'the men of old', but then, before he mentions any of them, he says something about the creation of the universe when, by definition, none of them were alive. What relevance therefore could this have to the subject in hand and to those addressed?

The answer to that question is provided by two parts of this verse. First, the writer uses the first person plural – 'we'. He is therefore speaking about himself and his readers, not the people of old. But, secondly, he uses the same language as in verses 1 and 2, speaking about the visible in relation to the invisible. The writer is therefore referring to the same faith as the elders had, but is doing so in terms of the faith that he and his readers share. What does he say?

He declares that a wonderfully-furnished world was not brought into being out of what was visible, that is, not from any pre-existent (eternal) matter, but by the all-creating Word of God, and that was something which they understood and believed. For them, God's Word was the more than sufficient explanation of the world that is. It was intellectually adequate and spiritually satisfying. It was the stuff of faith. Believing that, why should they have any difficulty, given God's Word, about believing in the existence and glory of an unseen world, a heavenly country and an eternal city which God has planned and made – a heavenly Jerusalem and a heavenly high priest (11:15–16; 12:22)?

Faith therefore has a sound basis and an irrefutable logic. It has a 'Word' and it 'understands'. It relates to what lies outside itself – a Word about 'a world' by which it understands; a promise from God which it 'sees', 'embraces' and 'confesses'. It is not irrational; it is not a flight from the real world. It is an understanding of the world – in the only way in which it can properly be understood, as a world that God has made and will re-make. It is not intellectual suicide and it is more than an intellectual assent. Faith is neither inward-looking nor self-sustaining.

It is just not reasonable to believe what is taught in Genesis 1 and 2, but not what is recorded in Revelation 21 and 22, and that applies the other way around too. The God who made a wonderful earth can make an even more wonderful heaven. No other could make either.

3. FAITH AND WORSHIP

Believing is worshipping God. It is in this connection that the first of the Old Testament 'elders' is named – Abel. What is said about his faith is related specifically to the quality of the sacrifice which he offered to God.

There are two views on why Abel's sacrifice was 'better'. Each has merit. The first is that Abel brought a blood sacrifice and Cain did not. The basis for this is that Genesis 4:4 refers not only to the firstlings of the flock but 'to their fat [portions]' and that implies that the animals have been slain. The explanation is therefore that Abel, knowing that he needed a covering for his sin, as had his parents, Adam and Eve (3:21; contrast 3:7), followed God's method of providing it in the worship he brought. So as a penitent sinner who knew his life was forfeit, he worshipped God in faith with the firstling lambs of his flocks. The second view sees the contrast between him and his brother as lying in their differing states of heart which were manifested in the lavishness or otherwise of their respective offerings. While each brought what was his own, Cain brought only 'of the fruit of the ground' (not even the first-fruits), whereas Abel brought the firstlings of his flock.

Whichever of these views is adopted, and either is possible, the important point to note is that faith manifests itself in worship of God according to his will. Today, the wide-spread idea is that whatever we devise qualifies as acceptable worship, and the dimension of worship being directed to God is being lost sight of. Instead of the vertical, something horizontal is cultivated, something done to make people feel good, rather than what pleases God; and it is only the latter that God will approve.

4. FAITH AND FELLOWSHIP

Believing is pleasing God. It is walking in fellowship with a living God. That is what Enoch did, the next 'elder' to be mentioned. It is important to note that verse 6, which speaks about 'coming to God', is to be connected with verse 5, with what is said about Enoch, before making use of it as a general truth. (It begins with 'and', and so verse 6 is a comment on or deduction from verse 5).

Enoch came to God regularly, daily, believing that he was alive (God 'is') and that he responded positively and abundantly to those who sought him (God is a 'rewarder'). Enoch therefore desired him as a companion and sought to please him wherever he went, and whatever he did. There was consequently something of an 'unseen world' about Enoch; and then, one day, he was nowhere to be found. There was no trace of him, Where had he gone? Death was not the explanation because no body was found. God 'took him up', body and soul. Fellowship with a living God triumphs over death.

5. FAITH AND ETERNITY

Believing involves condemning 'the world' and becoming 'an heir of righteousness'. So far, the fact of human sin has only been alluded to by the mention of sacrifice and death but what is now said about Noah has a fallen human race for its context. He believed God's Word to him about impending judgement and the means by which he and his family could be preserved in it and delivered out of it. Fear that consists of awe of God is compatible with faith. Indeed, a faith without reverence for God is no faith at all. In the same way, obedience which consists of submission to God is necessarily part of true faith. By building an ark Noah was saying two things. He was condemning the world; that is, he was endorsing God's sentence on fallen mankind. But he was also affirming God's way of salvation. He was trusting God's way of salvation, and so he was reckoned as being righteous by God. Faith believes in judgement as well as salvation, in hell as well as heaven.

22

Obtaining Promises

⁸ *By faith Abraham, when he was called, obeyed by going out to a place which he was to receive for an inheritance; and he went out, not knowing where he was going.* ⁹ *By faith he lived as an alien in the land of promise, as in a foreign land, dwelling in tents with Isaac and Jacob, fellow-heirs of the same promise;* ¹⁰ *for he was looking for the city which has foundations, whose architect and builder is God.* ¹¹ *By faith even Sarah herself received ability to conceive, even beyond the proper time of life, since she considered Him faithful who had promised;* ¹² *Therefore also there was born of one man, and him as good as dead at that, as many descendants as the stars of heaven in number, and innumerable as the sand which is by the seashore.* ¹³ *All these died in faith, without receiving the promises, but having seen them and having welcomed them from a distance, and having confessed that they were strangers and exiles on the earth.* ¹⁴ *For those who say such things make it clear that they are seeking a country of their own.* ¹⁵ *And indeed if they had been thinking of that country from which they went out, they would have had opportunity to return.* ¹⁶ *But as it is, they desire a better country, that is a heavenly one. Therefore God is not ashamed to be called their God; for He has prepared a city for them.* ¹⁷ *By faith Abraham, when he was tested, offered up Isaac, and he who had received the promises was offering up his only begotten son;* ¹⁸ *it was he to whom it was said, 'In Isaac your descendants shall be called.'* ¹⁹ *He considered that God is able to raise people even from the dead, from which he also received him back as a type.* ²⁰ *By faith Isaac blessed Jacob and Esau, even regarding things to come.* ²¹ *By faith Jacob, as he*

was dying, blessed each of the sons of Joseph, and worshiped, leaning on the top of his staff. ²² By faith Joseph, when he was dying, made mention of the exodus of the sons of Israel, and gave orders concerning his bones. ²³ By faith Moses, when he was born, was hidden for three months by his parents, because they saw he was a beautiful child; and they were not afraid of the king's edict. ²⁴ By faith Moses, when he had grown up, refused to be called the son of Pharaoh's daughter, ²⁵ choosing rather to endure ill-treatment with the people of God than to enjoy the passing pleasures of sin, ²⁶ considering the reproach of Christ greater riches than the treasures of Egypt; for he was looking to the reward. ²⁷ By faith he left Egypt, not fearing the wrath of the king; for he endured, as seeing Him who is unseen. ²⁸ By faith he kept the Passover and the sprinkling of the blood, so that he who destroyed the firstborn would not touch them. ²⁹ By faith they passed through the Red Sea as though they were passing through dry land; and the Egyptians, when they attempted it, were drowned. ³⁰ By faith the walls of Jericho fell down after they had been encircled for seven days. ³¹ By faith Rahab the harlot did not perish along with those who were disobedient, after she had welcomed the spies in peace. ³² And what more shall I say? For time will fail me if I tell of Gideon, Barak, Samson, Jephthah, of David and Samuel and the prophets, ³³ who by faith conquered kingdoms, performed acts of righteousness, obtained promises, shut the mouths of lions, ³⁴ quenched the power of fire, escaped the edge of the sword, from weakness were made strong, became mighty in war, put foreign armies to flight. ³⁵ Women received back their dead by resurrection; and others were tortured, not accepting their release, so that they might obtain a better resurrection; ³⁶ and others experienced mockings and scourgings, yes, also chains and imprisonment. ³⁷ They were stoned, they were sawn in two, they were tempted, they were put to death with the sword; they went about in sheepskins, in goatskins, being destitute, afflicted, ill-treated ³⁸ (men of whom the world was not worthy), wandering in deserts and mountains and caves and holes in the ground (Heb. 11:8–38).

To have more to say than time will allow is evidently not just the problem of present-day preachers – the preacher who wrote this letter knew something about this too (see verse 32). He realized that there was much more in the Old Testament that was relevant to his sermon than he could include in his survey. We must find some way of dealing with what he did mention within manageable limits.

To examine this large section stage by stage would be an immensely rewarding way of studying it, and also the corresponding Old Testament material. Doing that would prove that a harmony does exist between the Testaments, with respect not only to messianic predictions but also to biographical accounts, and it would supply a method for interpreting Old Testament narratives that are not referred to this chapter. Surely Caleb, who 'followed the LORD fully', ought to have been included in a chapter like this. But perhaps he was in the author's mind when he wrote the words, 'Who through faith obtained promises' (verse 33) – the words that give us the title for this study.

We will try to give prominence to the highly personal character of this chapter, because that is its recurring emphasis. The stylistic pattern which the writer follows can be reduced to the following: 'By faith someone did something as a result of which something else occurred.' This means that the writer is not just writing about history but about 'history-in-the-making'. 'By faith' things *happened* in time and space, and that on two levels. First, there is the level of a person's development as a believer – 'from weakness were made strong' (verse 34). This is growth in faith. Secondly, there is the plane of community-history, that is, the history of God's redeemed people – 'conquered kingdoms . . . put foreign armies to flight' (verse 34). That is the development of God's saving purpose. Trusting God to be as good as his Word produced a catalogue of personal achievements and 'ecclesiastical' advances. While some of these are miraculous, others are only striking providences; but all of them are both human triumphs and acts of God, often occurring in times of crisis and adversity.

In order to do justice, therefore, to what the writer records about faith we must not only assert that the individuals who believed God's revealed Word actually existed (to say they can really inspire

the living without having lived themselves is specious), but also try
to enter into what happened to them and to others as a result of
their believing God's Word. We must try to sit where each sat and
look at the situation through his or her eyes. What did 'believing'
really mean for them?

Our plan is to consider these verses by concentrating on
Abraham and Moses. All the others named are associated with one
or other of these towering figures and their significance in the Old
Testament, that is, either with 'the promise' (verse 10) or the
'Exodus' and entry into the land (verses 22–31). Joseph can be
regarded as linked with both in that he belonged to the age of the
patriarchs, but also to Israel's Exodus from Egypt and settlement in
Canaan which he predicted.

1. ABRAHAM

Verses 8 – 22 are the relevant verses here and Genesis 12–40 is the
section of the Old Testament which is being summarized. Isaac,
Jacob, Sarah and Joseph are those who are named, and what binds
them all together is 'the same promise' (see verse 9) as Abraham
received, that is, the covenant God made with Abraham. This is
shown by the fact that two of its pledges, namely, 'seed' and 'land',
are specifically mentioned in this section, and the third, 'the
nation', is alluded to in verse 12, which is a quotation from Genesis
15:5. All those named and unnamed believed that this triple
promise would be fulfilled in both its physical and its higher senses.
But they had to live and die without seeing the fulfilment of either
dimension of the promise. That is what characterized their times.
We will use 'the land' and 'the seed' as focal themes because the
nation is an extension of the latter.

i. *The Land*

This was never their possession. They lived in it, but as people
who never settled anywhere for long. Abraham and Sarah, Isaac
and Jacob were living in tents although they knew that the land
belonged to them by the promise of God and not to its occupants
who were at the time living in cities. They were 'strangers' where
they were, and 'pilgrims' to somewhere else, consciously so. What
is more, if an earthly territory had been the horizon of their

expectation, they would have given up and gone home, back to Ur of the Chaldees where they came from. But they were looking 'upward' to a better land and to a city that God had planned and constructed, and not merely forward to a time when they would possess the land on which they stood. This was the hope even of Joseph in the land of Egypt, who wanted his bones taken from Egypt when the Exodus occurred and the nation moved towards the Promised Land.

ii. *The Seed*

Two incidents are specified in connection with faith and 'the seed'. The first relates to Sarah and the second to Abraham. 'Death' was the context in which each believed in God. Sarah believed that she would have a child when she was past childbearing age, and Abraham was 'as good as dead' (verse 12). Abraham believed when that child was 'as good as dead' because he was about to sacrifice him at the command of God. A remarkable conception and a metaphorical resurrection were the result of believing that what God had promised he would give, and what he had given once, he was able to give again. It is impossible not to see here a type of the Messiah whose conception was miraculous and whose resurrection out of death was actual.

The believing attitude of these pre-Mosaic people is described by four verbs in verse 13 namely 'having seen', 'were persuaded', 'embraced' and 'confessed' (AV). They can form two pairs: to 'see' and 'be persuaded' describes reception of the promise; to 'embrace' and 'confess', their response to it. Clearly, the idea that the patriarchs knew very little of 'heart-religion' and nothing of gospel days finds little support here. They knew more than we often think they did. But they 'died in faith', that is, without having received all they hoped for, but not without having some of it before their eyes and more of it in their heart, and in the expectation of receiving it all. What is said about Jacob, Isaac and Joseph as they faced death shows that to be the case. 'Things to come' were in their minds and hearts, and they prophesied blessings that would come to future generations. Christians have had more made known to them than these forefathers. With the unseen world in view we should therefore live and die more confidently.

2. MOSES

The people named in verses 24–31 and the events mentioned there are all found in the books of Exodus to Joshua. They are grouped around the Exodus, the entry into the Promised Land, and its occupation. All of these events were set in the context of opposition. First, there was the power of Egypt. Then there were the residents of Canaan, summed up by the walls of Jericho, and the enemies of the judges and the kings, Assyria, Babylonia, Persia and Greece. The need to fight was the characteristic of those times, and it was done in faith. The patriarchs had walked by faith; the judges and the kings had to fight in faith. The story of opposition being resisted is continued with the list of enemies, men and beasts, fire and sword, mockings and scourgings, chains and imprisonment, impoverishment and torture. But believing in God won the day. The world regarded them as not worthy of belonging to its society. God regarded them as more than worthy of belonging to his city.

All this is summed up in what is said about Moses. He had to face Egypt, represented by 'the king's edict', the harsh bondage Pharaoh imposed, and the fear he inspired; the destroying angel, the Red Sea and the pursuing Egyptians. It was by faith that he met every challenge. For him all the splendour and wealth of Egypt could not even be compared with the lowly condition of the oppressed Hebrews because of the reward that was bound up with the coming of the promised Messiah from their race. In spite of his having been educated as an Egyptian, and having an exalted rank as the son of the daughter of Pharaoh, he refused that identity and became one of those with less than nothing in the world's eyes. He 'refused' what was visible; he 'chose' what was invisible; and he 'endured'.

But 'by faith' he not only faced the wrath of an earthly king, but a heavenly one. He saw a greater king than Pharaoh, one who was not visible to the naked eye and saw him as threatening Israel no less than Egypt if his appointed way of deliverance was not observed. So he kept the Passover and saw to it that the sacrificial blood was sprinkled on the lintels and the doorposts for the protection of the Israelites. He saw a nation judged and a nation spared.

Believing would consequently enable the Hebrews to endure a wait, and also a war, until the One whose coming was drawing near would be present and the promise would be fulfilled – to endure having nothing but life and to risk losing even that. With this perspective we can obtain that encouragement to wait with expectation for God to do his work as we keep his Word. Faith is not whistling in the dark, looking for a silver lining or a happy feeling. It is neither make-believe nor virtual reality, but is courageous. It faces reality, grim reality at times, before 'obtaining promises', when it will be more than vindicated.

23

Following the Forerunner

¹ Therefore, since we have so great a cloud of witnesses surrounding us, let us also lay aside every encumbrance, and the sin which so easily entangles us, and let us run with endurance the race that is set before us, ² fixing our eyes on Jesus, the author and perfecter of faith, who for the joy set before Him endured the cross, despising the shame, and has sat down at the right hand of the throne of God. ³ For consider Him who has endured such hostility by sinners against Himself, so that you will not grow weary and lose heart. ⁴ You have not yet resisted to the point of shedding blood in your striving against sin; ⁵ and you have forgotten the exhortation which is addressed to you as sons, 'My son, do not regard lightly the discipline of the Lord, nor faint when you are reproved by Him; ⁶ for those whom the Lord loves He disciplines, and He scourges every son whom He receives.' ⁷ It is for discipline that you endure; God deals with you as with sons; for what son is there whom his father does not discipline? ⁸ But if you are without discipline, of which all have become partakers, then you are illegitimate children and not sons. ⁹ Furthermore, we had earthly fathers to discipline us, and we respected them; shall we not much rather be subject to the Father of spirits, and live? ¹⁰ For they disciplined us for a short time as seemed best to them, but He disciplines us for our good, so that we may share His holiness. ¹¹ All discipline for the moment seems not to be joyful, but sorrowful; yet to those who have been trained by it, afterwards it yields the peaceful fruit of righteousness. ¹² Therefore, strengthen the hands that are weak and the knees that are feeble, ¹³ and make straight paths for your feet, so that the limb which is lame may not be put out of joint, but rather be healed. ⁴ Pursue peace with all men, and the sanctification without which no one will see the Lord. ¹⁵ See to it that no one comes short of the grace of God; that no root of bitterness springing up causes trouble, and by it many be defiled; ¹⁶ that there be no immoral or godless person like Esau, who sold his own birthright for a single meal. ¹⁷ For you know that even afterwards, when he desired to inherit the blessing, he was rejected, for he found no place for repentance, though he sought for it with tears (Heb. 12:1–17).

In reviewing Old Testament history in Chapter 11, the writer used the third person, giving his readers the opportunity to think about others and not themselves. But now he addresses them directly, depriving them of that luxury. Similarly, in a sermon, some diversion from direct speech is often welcomed by one's hearers and is beneficial provided it is not just a gap-filler, unconnected with the main theme. Hebrews 11 is certainly no digression! But now the preacher's tone changes and there is nowhere for anyone in 'the congregation' to hide. The writer uses the second person plural relentlessly as he once more exposes the Hebrews' condition and calls upon them to remedy it.

They have been presented with many examples of believing people in order to encourage them to a like faith. One more is added in these verses, but he is not just a believer, like them. He is 'Jesus the author and perfecter of faith'. He is therefore more than another example of what it means to live and die 'by faith'; he is the originator of his people's faith and the one who brings it to perfection. He is its beginning and end. He has been described as 'the author of their salvation' (2:10), that is, their champion in the fight with Satan and sin, and also their 'forerunner' (see 6:20) – the one who goes on before, opening up the way, so that it is safe for others to follow. They are therefore summoned to hold him in clear view (verse 2) and to 'consider' him, particularly with regard to the endurance he displayed (verse 3).

Everyone knows that athletic imagery is used in the opening verses of this chapter. What is not so obvious however is that this allusion never wholly disappears from the author's mind even though he uses other analogies: from family life in verses 8–10, and from the medical world in verses 12–13. When he writes about the Father's discipline he refers to gymnastics (verse 11), and in what he says about the healing of a limp he refers to a track or course (verse 14). The athletic analogy is therefore the dominant one in this passage as he describes a pursuit of peace and holiness which leads to the beatific vision of the Lord. We will survey these verses under the headings of *running the race, undergoing discipline* and *pursuing holiness*.

1. RUNNING THE RACE (verses 1–3)

A foot race in the ancient games supplies the illustration for all that follows. It is not a sprint, but more like a long-distance race, one that calls for stamina and not a short burst of energy. Jesus ran such a race and he finished the course, in spite of everything. He pressed on, setting aside all that would have hindered him from doing the will of God, being sustained by the prospect of what lay beyond it all. The shameful death of the cross and the snarling opposition of his foes were as nothing in comparison with the joy of heaven. In his struggle with sin he shed his blood. As he was nailed to the cross he thought of sitting at his Father's right hand. Eternity was more real to him than time.

This supplies the pattern and the power for the Hebrews in their race. Though they will encounter hindrances from their adversaries, they are not to add to them by difficulties of their own making. They were to lay aside everything that would have the effect of slowing them down or diverting their attention from the goal – even if it was not sinful in itself. Their indolence and fascination with Judaism, occasioned through the 'deceitfulness of sin' (3:13), are certainly included in this. They are to look away from everything to Jesus, even from the 'so great cloud of witnesses', who can only say that finishing the course is possible, whereas Jesus can sustain and perfect weak faith. They are therefore to fix their believing eyes on him and not them. Meditating on his dogged perseverance on earth and his present joy in glory will stiffen their resolve and give wings to their feet. So it will be with believers today. Those who overcome will sit with him on his throne. The New Testament Gospels and Epistles should be read no less than the Old Testament!

2. UNDERGOING DISCIPLINE (verses 4–13)

Learn and living are closely related. Theory is important, but only as a prelude to experience. The best way to really learn is by doing, or enduring. Jesus learned by suffering what he could not have learned by any other means. It led to his being 'made perfect' (see chapter 5:7-9). He submitted to training and he suffered being tempted, and so he became the author of life and the finisher of faith.

The Hebrews, on the other hand, were not learning or living but drifting. They were not in earnest, but were distracted and consequently dispirited. They were not benefitting from the Son, and so the discipline of the Father was called for. They were being pruned by the gardener (*John* 15:1) so that they brought forth more fruit – 'the peaceable fruit of righteousness' (see verse 11).

The writer quotes Proverbs 3:11–12 on this point because those verses emphasize the importance of discipline. They make clear that being disciplined is a proof of sonship, and that there are ways in which it should and should not be responded to. The Hebrews needed to hear all this – as Christians do today.

Earthly fathers go to greater lengths in training their own children than they do with those of others. Even when their discipline is not the best, it is an expression of love. But the discipline of the 'Father of spirits' is always for the good of his sons, so that they may live eternally. Its purpose is not only that he should be honoured in them but also that they should become holy like him.

But discipline has to be endured, and a sense of having displeased a loving parent is not easy to bear. It is worse than whatever punishment is meted out. Sin can easily rise and surface at such a time, and express itself against the training being given. There are two ways in which that happens. Both are mentioned here. They can be described as 'making light' and 'making heavy', that is, becoming dismissive of the Father's reproof, or devastated by it. Neither is the same as persevering in faith. The former is like running one's own course; the latter is like dropping out of the race.

The appropriate response to discipline is to be 'exercised' or 'trained' by it – a word which is taken from the world of the athletic games and which gives us our term 'gymnast'. This is what the Hebrews had not been doing (see 5:12). Discipline pinpoints a weakness, a spiritual 'lameness'. Exercise strengthens what is weak and so brings healing. Doing nothing causes muscle wastage and atrophy – in a spiritual sense. One can become permanently lame and also cause others to stumble. What is involved in such exercise?

3. PURSUING HOLINESS (verses 14–17)

The 'straight track' to the finishing tape is now described in words from Isaiah 35:3 and Proverbs 4:26–27. Taken together, they are a call to be strong in view of God's coming deliverance and to run in 'straight paths' towards it. This combination shows that there is harmony between Old Testament prophetic and wisdom literature. The prophets speak of the coming day of the Lord and the wisdom writers about how to live in the light of it. New Covenant wisdom and eschatology are what is being described. The book of Proverbs should therefore accompany the stranger in this world and the pilgrim on his way to heaven, no less than the rest of Scripture.

But it is a Christian congregation that is being called to the 'straight course', to paths of peace and not evil. The exhortation is therefore in the plural. Each professing believer has a duty to obey for himself (verse 14), but also to be on the lookout for anyone who is failing to keep up with the company on the move (verse 15). Such a person, or persons, could drop out of the race altogether, taking the fateful step which is described in verses 16 and 17. Here, however, there is no warning expressed. Instead, an obligation is placed on those that are 'strong' to help any that are 'weak'. Need should not pass undetected, help should be given, and the danger averted. Wavering Christians are not to be written off.

Two Old Testament passages are in view in verses 15–17. Both are taken from the Pentateuch. The first refers to someone departing from the covenant Lord to worship other gods and being totally indifferent to the effect of his defection on the congregation (*Deut.* 29:18–19). The second reference is to Esau and his preference for physical gratification (the seen and the felt) over the covenant blessing that spoke of the unseen and the future. Both these examples stand in marked contrast to those of Hebrews 11.

But present waverers are not to be identified with past defectors. They can be restored through the grace of God.

The call to pursue peace and holiness indicates that enduring is not something wholly negative. It does not merely involve resisting influences of a counter-culture and rejecting the errors of a false religion. It is not just drawing 'a line in the sand', but an active pursuit of what is good and right in the sight of God, for others and for oneself. It is to be done by 'putting off' sin and 'putting on' righteousness; it is 'lay[ing] aside' what is sinful and 'looking [in faith] to Jesus'. That is the course to the Celestial City from the City of Destruction, to heaven from a world of evil. Its goal is not just a sight of those who have gone before in faith, but of Christ himself.

24

In the Kingdom

¹⁸ For you have not come to a mountain that can be touched and to a blazing fire, and to darkness and gloom and whirlwind, ¹⁹ and to the blast of a trumpet and the sound of words which sound was such that those who heard begged that no further word be spoken to them. ²⁰ For they could not bear the command, 'If even a beast touches the mountain, it will be stoned.' ²¹ And so terrible was the sight, that Moses said, 'I am full of fear and trembling.' ²² But you have come to Mount Zion and to the city of the living God, the heavenly Jerusalem, and to myriads of angels, ²³ to the general assembly and church of the firstborn who are enrolled in heaven, and to God, the Judge of all, and to the spirits of the righteous made perfect, ²⁴ and to Jesus, the mediator of a new covenant, and to the sprinkled blood, which speaks better than the blood of Abel. ²⁵ See to it that you do not refuse Him who is speaking. For if those did not escape when they refused him who warned them on earth, much less will we escape who turn away from Him who warns from heaven. ²⁶ And His voice shook the earth then, but now He has promised, saying, 'Yet once more I will shake not only the earth, but also the heaven.' ²⁷ This expression, 'Yet once more,' denotes the removing of those things which can be shaken, as of created things, so that those things which cannot be shaken may remain. ²⁸ Therefore, since we receive a kingdom which cannot be shaken, let us show gratitude, by which we may offer to God an acceptable service with reverence and awe; ²⁹ for our God is a consuming fire (Heb. 12:18–29).

Little children are usually taught their names and addresses lest they should become lost. In these verses the Hebrews, who have been described as 'babes', are being reminded of where they belong because they have become so disorientated. They were unable to differentiate between Judaism and Christianity so as to recognize the superlative exclusiveness of the latter. That is a mark of alarming immaturity.

The writer has been labouring to clarify the Hebrews' thinking about the superiority of Christ so that they would not treat what was less, that version of Old Testament faith and practice which was current in their day, as if it were the best. This need to identify things properly was all the more pressing because so much of Judaism consisted in what was visible, and impressively so. But it was the invisible that was substantial and eternal; the visible was only symbolical and temporary. Similarly, in the Christian church today, fascination with visible things, not to mention preoccupation with them, from images to icons, symbols to smells, robes to ritual, is a sure sign that true spirituality is either absent or on the decline. All religions are not equally valid and good.

In this passage the writer deals with this problem, and more besides, by means of what he says about mountains. Now, what could be more real than mountains? Two are in view in this passage, Mount Sinai and Mount Zion, but there are several things about the ways in which the writer refers to them here that are worth noticing. First, he does not use the name 'Sinai', and only uses the word 'mountain' when he quotes from Exodus 19:12, although he describes it in unmistakable terms. Secondly, it is not the Zion in Jerusalem that he writes about but rather its counterpart, 'the city of the living God, the heavenly Jerusalem'. He is therefore not thinking about mountains as earthly localities, though both still exist, but as scenes of divine revelation. His description of Sinai is a description of God's self-disclosure there, and so is what he says about the heavenly Jerusalem.

In presenting features of God's self-revelation on each mountain, the writer's aim goes further than providing instruction. He has an intensely practical purpose. He wants to show the Hebrews what great privileges are theirs. In that way he underlines the exhortation that has preceded, and also paves the way for the one to follow. He is saying to the 'little children', 'Remember your address, where you belong and where you live! You have a wonderful identity and destiny!' We will review what he says about each mountain before considering the appeal which he makes.

1. REVELATION AT SINAI (verses 18–21)

The way in which God revealed himself to his people at Mount Sinai was sensual; it was visual, audible and even tangible. The mountain could be touched and the wind could be felt; the trumpet and voices could be heard, the blazing fire could be smelt and the gloomy darkness could be seen. But it was all so terrifying. And there was the threat that if even an animal touched the mountain it was to be killed, but from a distance, not by a human hand directly, for fear of contamination. What would then happen to any human being who transgressed? It was all so unbearable that the people desired God's voice to fall silent.

The climax of this summary is taken from Moses' experience after the incident of the golden calf (see *Deut.* 9: 19). When he appeared before such a God to intercede for the nation, even he was overcome with terror, although he was not personally guilty of the rebellion.

God's self-revelation to those who 'came to' Sinai therefore set up a distance between him and them and created a barrier, striking terror into their minds and hearts, in spite of the fact that they had been delivered from Egypt. Those are the features the writer stresses about the Old Covenant – distance from God and terror of him. That is what was still being portrayed in the temple and its worship.

2. REVELATION ON MOUNT ZION (verses 22–24)

The opening words emphasize that the Hebrews 'have come' to Mount Zion and not to Sinai. This corresponds to the negative 'have not come' in verse 18. But this translation, though accurate, does not convey the colour of the original word, which means 'to become a proselyte'. Conversion is therefore in view and the writer is reminding the Hebrews that, when they professed faith, it was not faith in the Old Covenant but in the New. And what a different world they were brought into! Instead of terror there was joy ('angels in festal array' may be the meaning in verse 22), and instead of distance there was nearness to God even though he was 'the Judge of all' and 'a consuming fire'! How is this possible?

The picture presented here is in keeping with what was said in the Old Testament about Zion – the place where God dwelt and where his people gathered for fellowship with him through sacrifice (*Psa.* 50:1–5). But it is an enhancement, or fulfilment, of it, because it is the result of the New Covenant, not the Old. Much of what was said about Zion by the Old Testament prophets, for example in Psalms 46 and 87 and Isaiah 25:6–26:6, could not be true of it as 'the present Jerusalem', but only of the 'Jerusalem above [which] is free' (*Gal.* 4:25–26). The initial fulfilment of these predictions about Zion is in the church that is 'our mother', with more to come in heaven, much more.

All this is because Jesus' blood, unlike Abel's, does not invoke God's judgment. Rather, it calls for 'better things', because in his death Christ exhausted the wrath of God on account of the sin of his people. With their names recorded in heaven's civic register from all eternity, and gathered through the gospel, cleansed and renewed by his death, they and those who have already finished the race and reached the goal form one community. Boundaries of time and space and even death are meaningless to those who are in fellowship with Jesus. The communion of the saints is a reality. The invisible world is a present delight.

3. ADMONITION AND ENCOURAGEMENT (verses 25–29)

'To whom much is given, of him shall much be required', is the principle that underlies the warning against defection and the call to thankful service expressed in this section. The writer has spoken like this before, and used the argument from lesser to greater to reinforce his address (see 2:1–4 and 10:19–31). There is however a note of finality about this exhortation because the writer refers to the twin facts that the Hebrews have heard a voice from heaven, not earth, and received a kingdom that cannot be shaken. He speaks negatively, by way of admonition, and positively, by way of encouragement, and we will follow the course he takes.

The admonition is related to possible defection from God's Word – the very same sin as has been referred to before in relation to Sinai (10:28) when God's Word through Moses shook the earth (*Psa.* 68:7–8). But though the writer is referring to the same sin, he is not referring to the same revelation. Here he refers to a voice from heaven and quotes from Haggai 2:6–7 and 21 which predict a future shaking of heaven and earth. What is this shaking and when will it take place?

Verse 27 helps with the answer to these questions. The writer deduces from the words, 'Yet once more', that a 'shaking' like that which occurred in connection with the inauguration of the Old Covenant at Sinai, will take place. It will remove everything that can be shaken, that is, 'created things', meaning here the earthly tabernacle and all the provisions for sacrificial worship. These were not intended to be permanent, they were only to remain until the 'time of reformation' when the 'good [better] things', which were 'to come', actually came. The shaking is the ending of the Sinaitic covenant.

But some things cannot be shaken. These are the 'heavenly things', which were the template for the tabernacle (and temple) and the sacrifices, and when those things came with the 'great high priest', something indestructible and permanent stood forth. The New Covenant is everlasting. It will stand the test of time and the coming again of the Saviour; the wreck of the world and the dawn of eternity. To refuse to hear this word from heaven is to 'turn a deaf ear', not only to God's voice, but to his Last Word.

But once more the writer follows admonition with encourage-ment. Having such a kingdom (and king), 'Let us . . .', he says, as he begins to map out the response that is appropriate to the bestowal of such privileges. Interestingly he uses thoughts and even words from Exodus–Deuteronomy to describe this. The Old Testament Scriptures have not been shaken and passed away! Nor has God – he is still a consuming fire to all who are unfaithful and depart from him (*Deut.* 4:24; see also *Heb.* 10:30) The new covenant calls for a life devoted to God in reverence and gratitude and obedience to his Word – and that applies in all the realms that are mentioned in the next chapter: the home and family, the world and business, the church and her worship and leadership.

25

Serving the King at Home

¹ Let love of the brethren continue. ² Do not neglect to show hospitality to strangers, for by this some have entertained angels without knowing it. ³ Remember the prisoners, as though in prison with them, and those who are ill-treated, since you yourselves also are in the body. ⁴ Marriage is to be held in honor among all, and the marriage bed is to be undefiled; for fornicators and adulterers God will judge. ⁵ Make sure that your character is free from the love of money, being content with what you have; for He Himself has said, 'I will never desert you, nor will I ever forsake you,' ⁶ so that we confidently say, 'The Lord is my Helper, I will not be afraid. What will man do to me?' (Heb. 13:1–6).

These verses and all that follows may seem to be made up of a number of exhortations that are quite unconnected with each other. Such a conclusion would be partly understandable because the chapter does not have an obvious structure. But it would be surprising if it were true, because our author has been so methodical in the way he has handled his material. A closer examination of the chapter shows that he is no less methodical here.

First, each of the four exhortations in verses 2–5 is connected with the 'love' which is mentioned in verse 1 in either positive or negative ways. Secondly, the reminder about past leaders in verse 7 is rounded off in verses 17–19 with a call for obedience to present leaders. Thirdly, and within that section, verses 9–16 concentrate on what differentiates Christian faith and life from Judaism and call for a final break from the latter. The connectedness of almost the whole of this chapter is therefore accounted for, apart from verses 20–25, which are made up of a doxology, a parting comment

[147]

and a benediction. Clearly our writer has not given free rein to random thoughts as he comes to the end of what he wants to say.

This receives further confirmation in two ways. First, there are many details in this final chapter that have already been majored on in the letter and so it forms a fitting conclusion to the whole. In addition to practical expressions of brotherly love (see 6:10 and 10:33–34), the writer mentions the preachers they had heard (see 2: 3); the changeless Christ (see 1:10–12); examples of faith (see 6:12–15 and 11:1–40); the ineffectiveness of animal sacrifices and the efficacy of the blood of Christ (see 9:9–10:4) and the pilgrim character of the people of God (see 3:12–4:11). The cluster of themes in the benediction also pick up on matters previously commented on, and exhortations previously given to 'remember' and 'continue' are repeated (see 10:32–39).

Finally, and overlooking the chapter division, there is a theme presented in 12:28–29 that can very naturally provide a heading for all that is contained in this closing chapter. It is *the kind of service that is appropriate in the unshakeable kingdom that God has introduced through Jesus Christ*. This is what provides us with a line of thought to integrate this and our closing study. We will think of serving the King in the variety of relationships and situations mentioned. But first of all we must identify the King.

1. The King

A kingdom is only as durable as its king, and it derives its character from him. Jesus, the Christ, is God's King, as the first chapter has informed us, and he is 'the same yesterday, today and forever' (verse 8). Just as his being 'begotten today' (see 1:5) does not refer to his eternal generation as the pre-incarnate Son, but to his enthronement as Messiah, so it is with his being 'the same . . . for ever'. This does not refer to his being co-eternal with God the Father but to his being changeless as the 'Christ', the last Prophet, the great King and High Priest. He will never be deposed or retire. He will never have a successor. His merit and resources will never diminish. He is ever full of gracious aid and ready to give it to his people. What he was 'yesterday' to the leaders who have finished their course, he is 'today' to the author and readers of this letter, and will continue to be 'forever' to his people in every time and place.

2. SERVING THE KING (verses 1–6)

The duties which are specified in these verses have the home situation as their most natural context, but not to the exclusion of the general social environment. That is how we will consider them. Four duties are mentioned in these verses. Each is not only stated clearly but is also strengthened by the addition of some reason to encourage compliance with it. They can all be viewed as related to the physical body in some way or other, although that may not have been a factor in the author's mind. It is certain, however, that the Christian message gives the body an honoured place. We will review them in pairs.

The first two are examples of love for others. First, there is *'brotherly love'*. That is not kindness to those of one's own family, or nationality, or even common humanity, but to fellow Christians. Two particular ways in which this can be shown are by providing *hospitality* for itinerant preachers and *support for those imprisoned* for the faith.

Hospitality was needed for those who itinerated in the cause of the gospel. It would not have been fitting for them to be accommodated overnight in local inns that were both dangerous and notorious places.

Similarly, those who were imprisoned had physical needs too. Prisons were harsh places and jailors were not noted for kindness. There was no social welfare, and even if there had been, Christians would have been the last to receive it.

Christians who are at liberty are to supply the needs of those who are not, and to do so with that genuine sympathy which characterized the High Priest himself. Meeting the temporal needs of fellow Christians was in keeping with his teaching (see *Matt.* 25:35–36).

But strangers were not to be turned away either. Giving hospitality to such was highly esteemed by both Greeks and Jews, so that it would be a terrible shame if Christians did less than others, or did so grudgingly. The writer encourages people to this duty by another reminder from the life of Abraham. He entertained three men, though not because he understood that they were heavenly visitors, and one of them turned out to be the LORD himself (*Gen.* 18:1–8).

Physical needs are still in view in the next two exhortations which relate to kinds of greed. Immorality and love of money often go together. In the first century, no less than today, immorality and materialism were rife and Christians were not immune from the epidemic.

The marriage bond is the provision of God. It is to be monogamous and permanent until death and it is the only context in which sexual union is wholesome and beneficial. To abuse the divine gift of heterosexual relations, whether before or after marriage, is not only to injure others and weaken the foundation of an ordered society, but also to invite the judgement of God. Fornication and adultery are no part of that holiness which leads on to seeing the Lord.

Coveting breeds discontent, and gaining what one desires does not bring contentment, although advertising often presents it as if it would. Gratification is not the path to satisfaction. For Christians to profess that they have 'better things', and yet to live in a way that seems to say that earthly things are better still, is a shameful contradiction.

The true and lasting source of contentment is in God – in his presence and provision. The promise quoted in verse 5 points to that. It is an echo of the repeated divine undertaking, 'I will be your God and you will be my people.' The quotation could be from Deuteronomy 31:5 where Moses assures the people of Israel that God would be with them in the Promised Land, or from Joshua 1:5 where the LORD himself gave the same assurance to Joshua after the death of Moses. As our writer makes a point of saying that God 'himself' made the promise, the latter text must be in view. God assures the Christian that contentment is to be found in him alone. It is typified by rest in the Promised Land after wandering in the wilderness. It is the soul coming home. It is rest *in* God, and *with* God. The emphatic way in which the promise is expressed (five negative particles!) not only outlaws any hesitation about whether it is true, but also invites an equally confident disposition and declaration by way of spirited and understanding response. This is expressed in words from Psalm 118:6–7. The Hebrews are to be as certain that they have all the help they need in God as he is that he will uphold and provide for them. We should be just as certain.

26

Serving the King in the Church

[7] Remember those who led you, who spoke the word of God to you; and considering the result of their conduct, imitate their faith. [8] Jesus Christ is the same yesterday and today and forever. [9] Do not be carried away by varied and strange teachings; for it is good for the heart to be strengthened by grace, not by foods, through which those who were so occupied were not benefited. [10] We have an altar from which those who serve the tabernacle have no right to eat. [11] For the bodies of those animals whose blood is brought into the holy place by the high priest as an offering for sin, are burned outside the camp. [12] Therefore Jesus also, that He might sanctify the people through His own blood, suffered outside the gate. [13] So, let us go out to Him outside the camp, bearing His reproach. [14] For here we do not have a lasting city, but we are seeking the city which is to come. [15] Through Him then, let us continually offer up a sacrifice of praise to God, that is, the fruit of lips that give thanks to His name. [16] And do not neglect doing good and sharing, for with such sacrifices God is pleased. [17] Obey your leaders and submit to them, for they keep watch over your souls as those who will give an account. Let them do this with joy and not with grief, for this would be unprofitable for you. [18] Pray for us, for we are sure that we have a good conscience, desiring to conduct ourselves honorably in all things. [19] And I urge you all the more to do this, so that I may be restored to you the sooner. [20] Now the God of peace, who brought up from the dead the great Shepherd of the sheep through the blood of the eternal covenant, even Jesus our Lord, [21] equip you in every good thing to do His will, working in us that which is pleasing in His sight, through Jesus Christ, to whom be the glory

forever and ever. Amen. ²² *But I urge you, brethren, bear with this word of exhortation, for I have written to you briefly.* ²³ *Take notice that our brother Timothy has been released, with whom, if he comes soon, I will see you.* ²⁴ *Greet all of your leaders and all the saints. Those from Italy greet you.* ²⁵ *Grace be with you all* (Heb. 13:7–25).

'Jesus Christ, the same yesterday, and today, and forever' is perhaps the best-known statement in the whole epistle. Some have regarded it as a kind of summary of the whole letter. While it could serve in that way, it is much more natural to note its connection with its immediate context, which is the church. Looked at in this way it will be seen that it follows a reference to the ministry of the leaders of a congregation and leads into a section that describes what is involved in following their example. Its meaning and bearing is therefore crucial for every congregation of the Lord's people and, by extension, for the whole church. It shows incontrovertibly that Jesus the Christ is the Head of the church. This has already been made clear in what is said about him in 3:1–6 and 10:20–21.

We will therefore consider these verses from the standpoint of their relevance to the corporate life of a Christian congregation. They have much to say to every church, in any time and place. They refer to its human leadership, to its worship (both of which, sadly, are often a battle-ground in the church today), and also to the environment in which it finds itself. We will think about the church's leadership, its environment, and its worship.

1. THE CHURCH AND HER LEADERSHIP
Just as every kingdom has its officials, the church has its officers. These are provided by King Jesus, not appointed by the state, and they are to go ahead of the people, marking out the path for others to tread. In doing that, they are like Jesus the forerunner, whom they follow, seeking to direct others to him, the changeless Christ, by their teaching and example. The leaders referred to in verse 7 have 'lived and died in faith', just as those in Hebrews 11, and they have left behind a good testimony. There is hardly anything that is more destructive than a public fall of a leader in the church.

The kind of leadership that is in view here is described as a life in keeping with speaking the Word of God and watching over people's souls. Speaking the Word of God refers not only to the matter of the message but also to the manner in which it is made known. It is not only declaring what is in agreement with God's own Word, but clarity and confidence in the directness with which it is presented, whether orally or in written form. This letter is a good example of this very thing, and also of what is involved in 'watching over souls'. It is not a domineering intrusiveness into people's lives, which denies Christian liberty and discourages Christian maturity, but a paternal care which gives people help when needed in running toward the goal, so that they do not step off the track and drop out of the race. Such pastoral direction is to be responded to gladly and positively so as to make the work of leaders a joy, not a burden, and also a source of benefit. The church is not a democracy and there should be no authority crisis or power struggles in it (!).

When leaders depart to their rest and reward, Jesus the Christ remains the same. Out of his resources he provides – and *Hebrews* is an example of that. The passing of godly men is not therefore to be regarded either as a time when a church is bereft or as an occasion to be seized upon as an opportunity for wholesale change. 'Imitate their faith', is what the preacher wrote, and not 'depart from it', nor 'adjust it' in order to be relevant to a changed environment. What Jesus, the Christ, was to those who have gone before, he will also be to those who follow in their steps.

2. THE CHURCH AND HER ENVIRONMENT

The church exists for God's glory. It is primarily a worshipping community which bears witness to God in the world by serving him. Its authentic character always comes to clear manifestation in the way in which it upholds his name and his gospel in its environment, especially in the face of another religion. This is what the writer is underlining here with reference to this congregation of Hebrews and to Judaism. If Jesus is the changeless Christ, then all teachings and practices that are 'strange', that is, alien to him, are to be resisted. Judaism is clearly different from Christianity and, that being so, every other religion is too. The truth of Christ is vital for the church. It acts as a circle, including all who believe it but keeping out all those who endorse another creed and code, for example, 'those who serve the tabernacle'.

The writer's message here emerges from what he says about the 'cross', the 'camp' and the 'city' and their related locations. The cross – that is what he is talking about although he does not use the term – is 'outside the camp'. This is, of course, an allusion to the fact that the carcases of the animals slaughtered on the Day of Atonement were taken outside the camp and burned there, the camp being regarded as holy. But the cross was outside the camp gate. Jesus atoned for sin outside the city of Jerusalem, and that means that atonement for sin is not to be found in Judaism.

The Christian congregation to which the Hebrews belonged must therefore be found outside the Jewish religious institution. She is the 'congregation in the wilderness' (*Acts* 7:38), but that is not a 'no man's land', a trackless waste. It is the way to a 'city' which is '(ever)lasting' and which is coming to meet those who leave the camp, willing to bear the 'shame' of Jesus. In being different from her environment, secular as well as religious, and in the way in which she has the cross and the city at the centre of her life, lies the power of the church's evangelistic ministry.

3. THE CHURCH AND HER WORSHIP

Just as in the wilderness God fed his people, so Christians are fed and sustained on their pilgrimage. They 'have an altar' and 'those who serve' in 'the tabernacle' in connection with food that provides no spiritual sustenance, have no rightful place there.

This 'altar' is not a reference to the Lord's *Supper* but to his *death*. Nothing is offered to God at the communion table, and that, by definition, is what happens at an altar. Instead of bread and wine, and what they signify, being offered to God by us, they, and what they seal, are offered to us by God. The altar referred to is Calvary, or rather it is Jesus' death which he there offered to God, once for all. To feast on him by faith brings the grace of God into the soul. It is food indeed, beneficial and nourishing.

So Christ is not presented to God in any sense in Christian worship. Rather, he presents to God all that Christians bring by way of worship, perfecting it by his merit and mediation. But all

sacrifices are not over. There are some that do please God, the end
and goal of all worship (verse 15). Sacrifices to remove one's sin are
finished with – Christ has died – but sacrifices because one's sin has
been removed are not. Grace gives birth to gratitude, and little
gratitude displayed shows little grace known (see *Luke* 7:40–50).
What are the sacrifices that please God? Four are mentioned.

i. *Thankful praise* – verse 15.
Hosea 14:3 is quoted here, and the use of the term 'fruit'
indicates that such praise must arise from the heart to be acceptable
to God. It does do so as surely as every good tree brings forth
good fruit, but is there not always room for more fruit-bearing,
especially as something which is continual and always explicitly
Christ-centred (notice the mention of *'his name'*) is called for?

ii. *Benevolent activity* – verse 16
Doing good to others and sharing with those in need is a
summary of true love, primarily to fellow-Christians, but not
exclusively to them. Doing good to all is pleasing to God because
he does good to all.

iii. *Obedience to and prayer for leaders* – verses 17–19
We have said that the church is not a democracy. It has leaders
and they have authority. But they are also under authority and rule
for the Head of the church, to whom they will give an account on
the day of judgement. They are therefore to ensure that their
decisions are arrived at in accord with Christ's Word, and they are
not to think that they are beyond the obligation to explain their
decisions to the people, who are to defer to them unless those
decisions are manifestly contrary to Scripture. And leaders are to
be prayed for! It is not only church members who want always to
act with a good conscience that is in accord with God's Word, but
the leaders as well. Following this guideline will result in many a
congregation being saved from disruption and anarchy.

'Such sacrifices' are to be given to God because they please him,
and they are to be sacrificial in spirit and kind, involving costly self-
denial. Thanksgiving and praise are more than due to him for 'so
great salvation'. Continuing care for fellow Christians in need is

not to be forgotten. Submission to godly leaders is part of one's submission to God. Prayer for them and all gospel ministers manifests a desire to see the kingdom of the Lord Jesus Christ extended.

4. CONCLUSION

The letter closes with a wonderful benediction-doxology. By the gospel, man's greatest good coincides with God's greatest glory. The precise point of the benediction is that God will equip believers, that is, make them complete. He will do this in 'every good thing', and that must include the writer's preaching by this letter, and their praying and obeying in the light of it. God has promised that he will work through these means by his Spirit. Prayer, practice and preaching will bring down his blessing, and that will be demonstrated by their doing what is 'pleasing in his sight'.

God has been described in a number of ways in this letter but there are two details mentioned about him in these verses which have not been mentioned before. First, he is 'the God of peace', and secondly, he 'brought up from the dead' the Lord Jesus Christ. Of course, what has been said about the exaltation of Jesus after his death necessarily includes his resurrection, but that does not mean that we have the right to overlook the specific mention of it here. The God of peace is the one who make people whole, even immature Christians, and the God who raises from death is one who has ultimate power. Peace and power are the hallmarks of the eternal covenant. God is able to do what will last 'forever and ever'. There is nothing too hard for him.

And so God will watch over his pilgrim people, his true church in the wilderness of this world, supplying them with all they need to the glory of his own name through Jesus Christ – a far better Shepherd of his sheep than even the unknown writer of this wonderful letter.

Group Study Guide

SCHEME FOR GROUP BIBLE STUDY
(Covering 13 Weeks)

	Study Passage	Chapters
1.	Hebrews 1:1–14	1–2
2.	Hebrews 2:1–18	3–4
3.	Hebrews 3:1–4:13	5–6
4.	Hebrews 4:14–5:10	7–8
5.	Hebrews 5:11–6:8	9–10
6.	Hebrews 6:9–7:10	11–12
7.	Hebrews 7:11–8:6	13–14
8.	Hebrews 8:7–9:12	15–16
9.	Hebrews 9:13–10:18	17–18
10.	Hebrews 10:19–11:2; 39–40	19–20
11.	Hebrews 11:3–38	21–22
12.	Hebrews 12:1–29	23–24
13.	Hebrews 13:1–25	25–26

This Study Guide has been prepared for group Bible study, but it can also be used individually. Those who use it on their own may find it helpful to keep a notebook of their responses.

The way in which group Bible studies are led can greatly enhance their value. A well-conducted study will appear as though it has been easy to lead, but that is usually because the leader has worked hard and planned well. Clear aims are essential.

AIMS

In all Bible study, individual or corporate, we have several aims:

1. To gain an understanding of the original meaning of the particular passage of Scripture;

2. To apply this to ourselves and our own situation;

3. To develop some specific ways of putting the biblical teaching into practice.

2 Timothy 3:16–17 provides a helpful structure. Paul says that Scripture is useful for:

(i) teaching us;

(ii) rebuking us;

(iii) correcting, or changing us;

(iv) training us in righteousness.

Consequently, in studying any passage of Scripture, we should always have in mind these questions:

What does this passage teach us (about God, ourselves, etc.)?

Does it rebuke us in some way?

How can its teaching transform us?

What equipment does it give us for serving Christ?

In fact, these four questions alone would provide a safe guide in any Bible study.

PRINCIPLES

In group Bible study we meet in order to learn about God's Word and ways 'together with all the saints' *(Eph.* 3:18). But our own experience, as well as Scripture, tells us that the saints are not always what they *are* called to be in every situation – including group Bible study! Leaders ordinarily have to work hard and prepare well if the work of the group is to be spiritually profitable. The following guidelines for leaders may help to make this a reality.

Group Study Guide

Preparation:

1. Study and understand the passage yourself. The better prepared and more sure of the direction of the study you are, the more likely it is that the group will have a beneficial and enjoyable study.
Ask: What are the main things this passage is saying? How can this be made clear? This is not the same question as the more common 'What does this passage "say to you"?', which expects a reaction rather than an exposition of the passage. Be clear about that distinction yourself, and work at making it clear in the group study.

2. On the basis of your own study form a clear idea *before* the group meets of (i) the main theme(s) of the passage which should be opened out for discussion, and (ii) some general conclusions the group ought to reach as a result of the study. Here the questions which arise from 2 Timothy 3:16–17 should act as our guide.

3. The guidelines and questions which follow may help to provide a general framework for each discussion; leaders should use them as starting places which can be further developed. It is usually helpful to have a specific goal or theme in mind for group discussion, and one is suggested for each study. But even more important than tracing a single theme is understanding the teaching and the implications of the passage.

Leading the Group:

1. Announce the passage and theme for the study, and begin with prayer. In group studies it may be helpful to invite a different person to lead in prayer each time you meet.

2. Introduce the passage and theme, briefly reminding people of its outline and highlighting the content of each subsidiary section.

3. Lead the group through the discussion questions. Use your own if you are comfortable in doing so; those provided may be used, developing them with your own points. As discussion proceeds, continue to encourage the group first of all to discuss the significance of the passage (teaching) and only then its application (meaning for us). It may be helpful to write important points and applications on a board by way of summary as well as visual aid.

[159]

4. At the end of each meeting, remind members of the group of their assignments for the next meeting, and encourage them to come prepared. Be sufficiently prepared as the leader to give specific assignments to individuals, or even couples or groups, to come with specific contributions ('John, would you try to find out something about Melchizedek for the next meeting?' 'Fiona, would you see what you can find out about how Psalm 95:7–11 is used by the writer of Hebrews?').

5. Remember that you are the leader of the group! Encourage clear contributions, and do not be embarrassed to ask someone to explain what they have said more fully or to help them to do so ('Do you mean . . . ?').

Most groups include the 'over-talkative', the 'over-silent' and the 'red-herring raisers'! Leaders must control the first, encourage the second and redirect the third! Each leader will develop his or her own most natural way of doing that; but it will be helpful to think out what that is before the occasion arises! The first two groups can be helped by some judicious direction of questions to specific individuals or even groups (*e.g.*, 'How do those who are not working outside of the home apply this?' 'Jane, you know something about this from personal experience . . .'); the third by redirecting the discussion to the passage itself ('That is an interesting point, but isn't it true that this passage really concentrates on . . . ?'). It may be helpful to break the group up into smaller groups sometimes, giving each subgroup specific points to discuss and to report back on. A wise arranging of these smaller groups may also help each member to participate.

More important than any techniques we may develop is the help of the Spirit enabling us to understand and to apply the Scriptures. Have and encourage a humble, prayerful spirit.

6. Keep faith with the schedule; it is better that some of the group wished the study could have been longer than that others are inconvenienced by it stretching beyond the time limits set.

7. Close in prayer. As time permits, spend the closing minutes in corporate prayer, encouraging the group to apply what they have learned in praise and thanks, intercession and petition.

STUDY 1: Hebrews 1:1–14

AIM: To see how God has spoken his last word in his Son.

1. The Old Testament is as much God's speech as the New. In what ways can we forget this?

2. Is Jesus as divine as God? Or is he just a special angel or super-prophet?

3. Look up some verses in both Testaments where the word 'glory' is found. Whose glory do they refer to, and what can we learn from them?

4. The Bible is complete, but does this mean it can become outdated? Or is it always contemporary?

5. How should we think of Jesus in relation to our physical world and the supernatural realm?

6. The Holy Spirit is referred to in verse 9 in connection with the Son as Messiah and his relationship with his people. What does this teach us about the church, as an organism and as an organization?

FOR STUDY 2: Read Hebrews 2:1–18 and chapters 3 and 4 of the text.

STUDY 2: Hebrews 2:1–18

AIM: To appreciate the greatness of God's salvation more, so that we do not drift away from it.

1. Christians need to appreciate the greatness of God's salvation more. What can help them to do this? What can hinder them?

2. The truth of the gospel has been confirmed in various ways down through the ages. What kind of confirmation of it is needed or possible today?

3. How can we make sure that we do not drift?

4. Today there is great interest in the supernatural, in possible beings on other planets, in stars, spirits and angels, both good and bad, and their influence on human life. What does this passage teach us about the place of human beings in a vast universe?

5. If Jesus had to be made like us and tempted like us to be our High Priest, should we not place more emphasis on his humanity than we do?

6. Why do people fear death? How can that fear be removed?

FOR STUDY 3: Read Hebrews 3:1–4:13 and chapters 5 and 6 of the text.

STUDY 3: Hebrews 3:1–4:13

AIM: To consider Jesus, our Apostle and High Priest, and the rest he provides.

1. Why is it important to make a distinction between the apostles of Jesus and those who are not apostles? *Both - prophet, priest King (Moses & Jesus); Jesus reality of picture*

2. What is involved in professing faith in the Lord Jesus Christ? *professing He is Apostle: High Priest (sent as apostle to intercede b/f*

3. How can we 'consider' the Lord Jesus? *pay attention to Him/who He is what He said Father - p marks scri*

4. 'God's Word is as timeless as it is timely.' Do you agree?

5. Should Sunday mean more to Christians than it does?

6. To be at rest is a universal and perennial longing. Where do people look for rest? Why can they not find it anywhere else but in God?

FOR STUDY 4: Read Hebrews 4:14–5:10 and chapters 7 and 8 of the text.

STUDY 4: Hebrews 4:14–5:10

AIM: To learn more of the Lord Jesus Christ as our great High Priest.

1. When we are in need, do we immediately think of going to our High Priest for help?

2. Have Christians ceased to think about the High Priesthood of Jesus as much as they should? Why do you think that this is the case?

3. Should more emphasis be placed on the High Priesthood of Jesus in the ministry of the Word in the church, and in the church's witness in the world?

4. What should we learn from Jesus' tears in Gethsemane (*Heb*.5:7)?

5. 'A salvation that is *complete* means that there is nothing more to be done. A Saviour who is *replete* means that there is much more to be given.' What are the implications of this for us?

6. Can we imagine that any need which a believer has will be unmet? If not, should we not be full of confidence?

FOR STUDY 5: Read Hebrews 5:11–6:8 and chapters 9 and 10 of the text.

STUDY 5: Hebrews 5:11–6:8

AIM: To consider the need to go on to perfection, or maturity.

1. *Perfection* or *perdition*: Is there a third possibility?

2. Why is belief in everlasting punishment declining among evangelical Christians?

3. Can a Christian grow without effort on his part, or without the aid of the Holy Spirit? What is the relationship between these two?

4. Is a grievous sin the same as apostasy?

5. Does apostasy involve a renunciation of Christian doctrines?

6. How would you help someone who, having made a Christian profession, believes that he or she has become an apostate?

FOR STUDY 6: Read Hebrews 6:9–7:10 and chapters 11 and 12 of the text.

STUDY 6: Hebrews 6:9–7:10

AIM: To benefit from the encouragement given in this passage.

1. Is God changeless? How does this encourage us?

2. Is God's justice ever a source of hope?

3. Which do you think is easier: to believe a promise, or to fulfil a command? Why?

4. 'Old Testament types were first symbols of truth to Old Testament people.' Do you agree?

5. Is it not striking that a King and a Priest, righteousness and peace, were to be found in Jerusalem long before the nation of Israel became the people of God ?

6. In what ways is the reign of Jesus as King resisted in the church today?

FOR STUDY 7: Read Hebrews 7:11–8:6 and chapters 13 and 14 of the text.

STUDY 7: Hebrews 7:11–8:6

AIM: To benefit further from the unchanging priesthood and ministry of the Lord Jesus Christ.

1. Did God change his mind between the two Testaments? How would you prove his changelessness from Scripture?

2. 'We should not confuse God's consistency with predictability.' Do you agree?

3. In what ways do we limit God in our thinking?

4. In one place in the New Testament, Jesus is described as standing at the right hand of God. How does this relate to the teaching of this passage about his being seated there?

5. Are you glad that we do not have a High Priest on earth? If so, why?

6. Can we learn something about how to help others to a better understanding of divine things from the way in which the writer argues in Hebrews 8:1–6?

FOR STUDY 8: Read Hebrews 8:7–9:12 and chapters 15 and 16 of the text.

STUDY 8: Hebrews 8:7–9:12

AIM: To gain a better understanding of why the New Covenant is better than the Old.

1. What is a covenant?

2. Why is it wrong to think of the Sinaitic covenant as only a covenant of law?

3. Under the New Covenant, what are the consequences when Christians sin? What does not and cannot happen?

4. F rom the relevant passages in the books of Moses, find out what each piece of furniture in the Tabernacle was meant to symbolize. What is the equivalent of each under the New Covenant?

5. In what other ways was the Holy Spirit active in Old Testament times?

6. Does the coming of the 'reformation' (*Heb*. 9:10) have any bearing on church architecture?

FOR STUDY 9: Read Hebrews 9:13–10:18 and chapters 17 and 18 of the text.

STUDY 9: Hebrews 9:13–10:18

AIM: To see how the one sacrifice of Christ is better than the many sacrifices of the Old Covenant, in itself and in its effects.

1. When we think of Christ's death, do we think of a sacrifice offered to God for sinners, or of a selfless gift offered to human beings?

2. Did Jesus accomplish everything by dying, or did he leave something for someone else to do – a sinner, for example, or a priest acting on his behalf?

3. Should a church committed to the gospel engage in joint communion services with churches which are not so committed?

4. 'Christianity is not only a *revealed* religion but an *experiential* one, with "miracles" in the heart and conscience.' Do you agree?

5. Could we be saved if God's will had not been done?

6. 'Our assurance of salvation by God's Son comes from God's Spirit.' Do you agree?

FOR STUDY 10: Read Hebrews 10:19–11:2 and 11:39–40; and chapters 19 and 20 of the text.

STUDY 10: Hebrews 10:19–11:2 and 11:39–40

AIM: To realize the need to persevere, like those who have gone before us in the faith.

1. The principle, 'The greater the privilege, the greater the responsibility', applies to Christians as well as to unbelievers. Have we taken seriously enough the idea of Christian duty?

2. How important are praying, caring for each other, and maintaining the faith in your church life?

3. Do we think of the Lord's coming as near any more? Should we?

4. Does the Old Testament teach a different way of salvation from the New?

5. Many biblical words are used so often that we do not always think of what they mean. What is faith? Describe it in your own words.

6. Only two women are named in Hebrews 11 (though others are mentioned). One of these is Rahab, a Canaanite. What does this teach about God's grace and the composition of the church? Do you see Rahab as your sister in the Lord?

FOR STUDY 11: Read Hebrews 11:3–38 and chapters 21 and 22 of the text.

STUDY 11: Hebrews 11:3–38

AIM: To grasp the nature of real believing, as seen in the lives of those described in this chapter.

1. 'Faith is not just *feeling*; it is not just *fact*; it is *fact felt.*' Do you agree?

2. Will God's revelation about creation and history ever be proved untrue? If it could, what would become of salvation?

3. Is the theory of biological evolution as serious a danger to the church as the teaching of conditional immortality?

4. What have you personally overcome by believing in God and his Word?

5. What is meant by 'a better resurrection' (*Heb.* 11:35)?

6. What evidence is there in the Book of Judges as to why Samson should be included in this chapter?

FOR STUDY 12: Read Hebrews 12:1–29 and chapters 23 and 24 of the text.

STUDY 12: Hebrews 12:1–29

AIM: To gain encouragement to 'run the race', and receive 'a kingdom which cannot be shaken'.

1. Do we think of Jesus as our Example? Should we? Are there any dangers in doing so?

2. What did Jesus endure?

3. Do we think enough about 'the joy set before us'? Has the reality of heaven tended to drop out of our thinking?

4. Should we beware of too much prominence being given to the visual in worship? Are any 'visual aids' appointed by Christ for his people's worship of God? Do you see any dangers even in those?

5. Do you believe in 'the communion of saints'? What do you understand by this term?

6. Do you see any conflict between what is said here about the heavenly Jerusalem and the teaching that a monarchy, a temple and sacrifices will again be established in Jerusalem on the earth?

FOR STUDY 13: Read Hebrews 13:1–25 and chapters 25 and 26 of the text.

STUDY 13: Hebrews

AIM: To learn more of the kind of service
the kingdom into which Christ has brought

1. Why does Christianity give such a place o
body in what it teaches? In what ways do Christia
take this more seriously?

2. 'Caring for the physical needs of Christians is a grand way to manifest and promote church unity, and to relieve the needs of unbelievers is vital to effective evangelism.' Do you agree?

3. Should Christians be equally concerned about *discontent* and *doubt*, and act against both with equal vigour?

4. Can a church be obeying its King if it does not prayerfully seek a minister of the Word? What makes a church content without a pastor, and should a church feel content just because it has one?

5. How can our participation in the Lord's Supper be improved, so that more of God's gracious blessing is received?

6. If the Christian church is to be as different from Judaism as this passage teaches, even though much of Judaism was appointed by God, can it be right for her to co-operate in inter-faith worship and missions?

REVIEW: Read through as much of Hebrews as possible at one sitting and write down the main lessons you have learned.